PRAYER GUIDE FOR SPIRITUAL EXPLOITS

The Saints Spiritual Security and Deliverance

MICHAEL A. OLADUNJOYE

Prayer Guide for Spiritual Exploits
Copyright © 2019 by Micheal A. Oladunjoye
All rights reserved.

Requests for information should be addressed to:
micholadunjoye@gmail.com

This book, or parts thereof, may not be reproduced, stored in a retrieval system, or transmitted in any form or by any means, electronic, mechanical, photocopying, recording or otherwise, without the written permission of the publisher.

Scriptures marked KJV are taken from the KING JAMES VERSION (KJV): KING JAMES VERSION, public domain.

Scriptures marked NKJV are taken from the NEW KING JAMES VERSION (NKJV): Scripture taken from the NEW KING JAMES VERSION®. Copyright© 1982 by Thomas Nelson, Inc.
Used by permission. All rights reserved.

Scriptures marked AMP are taken from the AMPLIFIED BIBLE (AMP): Scripture taken from the AMPLIFIED® BIBLE, Copyright © 1954, 1958, 1962, 1964, 1965, 1987 by the Lockman
Foundation Used by Permission

Scriptures marked CEV are taken from the CONTEMPORARY ENGLISH VERSION (CEV):
Scripture taken from the CONTEMPORARY ENGLISH VERSION copyright© 1995 by the American Bible Society. Used by permission.

Scriptures marked NIV are taken from the NEW INTERNATIONAL VERSION (NIV):
Scripture taken from THE HOLY BIBLE, NEW INTERNATIONAL VERSION ®. Copyright©
1973, 1978, 1984, 2011 by Biblica, Inc.™. Used by permission of Zondervan

Published By: Achievers World Publishing

ISBN: 978-0-6486778-2-6 (paperback)
ISBN: 978-0-6486778-3-3 (ebook)

Printed in Australia

DEDICATION

To the glory of the Almignty God and the LORD Jesus Christ who called, chose, and gave me the vision. He remains the great motivator for this book.

ACKNOWLEDGMENTS

My reverend worship and special appreciation to the Most High God for sending Jesus Christ at the fullness of time into my life to save my soul, open my eyes, as well as call and choose me for His purpose; to the LORD Jesus Christ, the author of life for giving me the vision and revelation; to the Holy Spirit for the capacity to write and complete this book despite all the compelling factors.

My gratitude also goes to the following people:

My mentor, Dr. D.K. Olukoya, President and Mentor, Goshen Club International for the fire of prayer kindled in me through the Apostolic Fire conferences and the Prayer and Deliverance Bible authored by him.

My wife, Deaconess Victoria Omolola Oladunjoye, my children, Adeyemi and Olawumi Adesanya; Afolabi and Tonbra Oladunjoye; Oluwole and Temidayo Oduneye; Olugbenga and Abisola Eleshinnla; also, to my grandchildren for their encouragement and support in one form or the other and at one time or the other during the process of actualizing this project.

My brothers in Christ, Bayo Adesanya and Pastor Femi Oyewopo for their counsel, inspiration, motivation and especially the efforts to make the project see the light of the day.

My friends, colleagues, children in the Lord, and a host of well-wishers touched by practical ministrations — thank you for the inspiration received through your testimonies and advice to put the knowledge into writing.

It is my sincere hope that, to a large extent, this book fulfils your most valued expectation.

Michael Akin. Oladunjoye

PREFACE

There is no way any book on prayer can claim absolute perfection. The best that can be claimed is that the book is perfect, good, hot, potent or effective but not absolute. I say this because prayer is talking to God about our needs in different ways: praise, worship, thanksgiving, supplication or intercession. It also takes various formats without set rules, patterns or ways of presentation.

When a book on prayer is written to fulfil a purpose and destiny, there is little fear about the format, rule or pattern. The objective is to present the prayers therein as they are revealed. This book, therefore, approaches prayers in line with the pattern in which they were revealed and presented in practical life ministrations.

The cardinal point to emphasize here is that if you intend to pray, try to do it according to the revelation received. When it agrees with the Word of God, leave the answer and supernatural intervention to God Almighty. Also, and most importantly, the person who intends to pray must ensure he or she is in right standing with God. Words of wisdom say, "It is not possible for God to use you as lighthouse anywhere if He cannot use you as candle where you are now."

I hope you will follow the approach taken in this book to achieve the success in your life, which was received and recorded by those who used these prayers in the past. Anyone who sincerely and faithfully applies these prayers to any need in life can succeed.

Michael Akin. Oladunjoye

Table of Contents

Introduction 1

Prayer 1: Receiving Divine Power For Great Exploits.... 6

Prayer 2: Have Mercy On Me, O Lord 10

Prayer 3: Set My Faith On Fire, O Lord 15

Prayer 4: God's Miracles Or Blessings Are
As Large As Your Faith 19

Prayer 5: Teach My Hands To War And My
Fingers To Fight, O Lord! 23

Prayer 6: Prevailing In Battles 27

Prayer 7: Look Up, Help Is Coming. 31

Prayer 8: Courage In Troubled Times.......................... 35

Prayer 9: There Is Hope For You
(You Are Not Hopeless) 40

Prayer 10: Do Not Give Up On Me.
Wake Up My Helpers To Help Me, O Lord 44

Prayer 11: Show And Lead Me In The Right Way,
O Lord 48

Prayer 12: Open My Eyes To See Your Well
Of Blessings, O Lord 52

Prayer 13: Forget The Past And Prepare For
New Things 56

Prayer 14: Flesh In My Life Must Die 60

Prayer 15: Touch Me With Your Healing Hand, O Lord 65

Prayer 16: Fix The Potholes Of My Life, O Lord 69

Prayer 17: Jesus Will Mend Your Broken Life 73

Prayer 18: Destroy The Work Of Evil Re-Creators In My Life, O Lord 77

Prayer 19: Evil Dreams In My Life Shall Be Aborted 82

Prayer 20: Wipe Out Every "But" In My Liffe, O Lord 86

Prayer 21: Receiving Power For Wealth And Prosperity 91

Prayer 22: Deliver Me From The Mentality Of "Not Enough" And "Not At All," O Lord 95

Prayer 23: Meet My Needs, O Lord! 100

Prayer 24: Recovering All The Enemies Have Stolen 105

Prayer 25: Break The Teeth Of The Ungodly In My Life, O Lord 110

Prayer 26: Break The Curse Of Failure And Poverty, O Lord 113

Prayer 27: Walking Out Of The Fire Of Affliction 117

Prayer 28: Evil Patterns In My Life Must Expire 121

Prayer 29: Evil Transactions Over My Life Shall Fail 125

Prayer 30: Wilderness Wanderings In My Life Shall Expire 129

Prayer 31: My Destiny, Come Out Of The Valley Of Suffering.. 133

Prayer 32: Enemies Of My Joy And Happiness Shall Be Disgraced And Silenced 137

Prayer 33: Evil Soul-Ties In My Life Must Be Broken 142

Prayer 34: Bring Disgrace And Destruction Upon My Accusers, O Lord! 147

Prayer 35: Break The Staff And Scepter Of Wicked Rulers In My Life, O Lord! 151

Prayer 36: Expose And Frustrate The Evil Agenda Of My Adversaries, O Lord! 155

Prayer 37: Deliver My Finances And Barricade Them From Satanic Onslaught, O Lord!....................... 159

Prayer 38: Every Haman In My Life Must Die 163

Prayer 39: Spoil My Spoilers, O Lord 167

Prayer 40: Settle Me, O Lord!..................................... 170

Prayer 41: Break In Pieces The Gates Of Brass Before Me, O Lord!.. 174

Prayer 42: Destroying The Devourers Of
My Harvest 178

Prayer 43: Disgrace The Evil Contenders
Of My Destiny... 182

Prayer 44: Roll Away Every Object Of Hindrance,
Limitation, And | Stagnation In My Life,
O Lord! 186

Prayer 45: Bring Me Out Of Every Humiliation
Of Man, O Lord! 190

Prayer 46: Break The Curse Of Failure In My
Earnest Expectation In You, O Lord! 194

Prayer 47: Frustrating Satanic Arrows 198

Prayer 48: Pulling Down The Habitation
Of The Wicked 202

Prayer 49: Hide Me From The Scourge
Of The Tongue, O Lord................................ 206

Prayer 50: Make Me Into A New Sharp
Instrument For Your Service, O Lord 210

Prayer 51: As Your Battle Axe And Weapon
Of War, Renew Me, O Lord! 213

Prayer 52: Overrule And Cancel The Judgment
Of The Wicked Over My Life, O Lord! 216

Introduction

"And call upon me in the day of trouble: I will deliver thee and thou shall glorify me"

(Psalm 50:15, KJV).

"He sent his word, and healed them, and delivered them from their destruction."

(Psalm 107:20, KJV).

Miracles are the supernatural work of God in the lives of human beings and the result of God's covenant with His people. They permeate the entire length and breadth of the Bible. In some cases, they happened because of God's intervention in people's lives. In other cases, they were done by God's anointed servants. It can be stated confidently that the entire Bible is the account of God's miracles in the world. The miracles of healing and deliverance in the Old Testament, as well as the New Testament, remain outstanding to the extent that they cannot be easily whisked away.

Miracles clearly identified the ministry of Jesus Christ and His apostles. It is also gratifying to note that these miracles have not ceased but are being carried on by God's faithful and anointed servants to fulfil the instructions of Christ.

The original plan of God for the human beings He created was for them to live in prosperity (general well-being) (Genesis 1:26-29). Shortly after the creation, the Devil appeared on the scene, deceived the people, and robbed them of the covenant of prosperity. The Devil and his demons (fallen angels) together with his human agents became the source of all evil, wickedness, and bondage in the world. Idolatry, occultism, witchcraft, and other vices have deeply rooted the world in problems. Therefore, the evil powers created themselves into powers behind these problems.

No human being is created to be above problems, affliction, and sorrow. Hence, it is not strange to discover that virtually every effort of human beings to find success, victory, joy, and peace has been filled with struggles and suffering. In the past, people have involved the patronage of herbalists, the occult, and other spiritual consultants hoping to find solutions.

Jesus Christ Himself knows that a great number of the people in the world have problems, which include the bondage of sin, ignorance, unbelief, demonic and witchcraft powers, vices, poverty, sickness or infirmity, curses and covenants to mention but a few. Out of His sincere desire and love to set free as many as are willing from evil bondage or captivity, He came to the earth, ministered deliverance and healing to people and, indeed, gave His life to set them free. The purpose of salvation, therefore, is for people to be delivered from the power of darkness and translated into the kingdom of God's Son, Jesus Christ (Colossians 1:13). From the moment He appeared on the scene, Jesus Christ has been searching for people to choose, anoint, and send forth as His instruments to liberate people in bondage.

> *And he said unto them, Go ye into all the world, and preach the gospel to every creature. He that believeth and is baptized shall be saved; but he that believeth not shall be damned. And these signs shall follow them that believe; in my name shall they cast out devils; they shall speak with new tongues; They shall take up serpents, and if they drink any deadly thing, it shall not hurt them; they shall lay hands on the sick, and they shall recover. So then after the Lord had spoken unto them, he was received up into heaven and sat on the right hand of God. And they went forth, and preached everywhere, the Lord working with them, and confirming the word with signs following, Amen.* **(Mark 16:15-20)**

The church, established by Jesus Christ, is made up of saints (believers) equipped with the power of the Holy Spirit to continue Jesus' work in the world. For the duration of Jesus Christ's ministry on the earth, He demonstrated God's power through the miracles, signs, and wonders done by

Him (Acts 10:38). At the time of His departure, He gave those who believed in Him the power to continue the work and promised to be with them (Matthew 28:20). Jesus instructed the disciples to preach the gospel to all people. Those who believed were added to the church. When they prayed or were prayed for by faith in the Word of God, which they heard, the challenges in their lives disappeared through miracles, signs, and wonders. Thus, believers in Christ (Christians) were clearly identified by preaching the gospel, prayers, miracles, signs, and wonders.

It is my strong belief that my call into the ministry, choice, and commission by Jesus Christ to deliver His people is to fulfil His desire and love. Therefore, it is not strange as part of the anointing received that I proffer and set out here in writing the platform for power and faith-filled prayers, which are necessary to do exploits for Christ.

For anything done in the realm of prayers to be effective and achieve the desired end of deliverance and healing, the person praying must have the presence of the following:

1. Holy Spirit
2. The Word of God
3. The name and blood of Jesus
4. And most importantly, faith to do the work

Specifically, the Holy Spirit is the power of God to do all things that are of God and Christ – for evangelism unto salvation, deliverance, and healing. The Word of God is the declared counsel of God. The name and blood of Jesus are two powerful elements in the work of redemption and faith. Faith is described as the thing that makes what we hope for real. It is proof of what we cannot see. Faith is believing what God says He will do even though the prevailing circumstances do not indicate the possibility. Faith is a "gift," which grows as it is exercised. Thus, faith is a very important aspect of a believer's life and powerful for results in the ministry of deliverance and healing.

In this prayer manual, an attempt is made to cover as many aspects of human life as possible. Even though human needs, trials, temptations, and sufferings are often intense and seem to last for eternity, approaching them in the right way and with the proper instruments will ensure the desired results. God is incomparable in power, strength, mercy, and faithfulness. He is omnipotent (all-powerful), omniscient (knows all things), and omnipresent (in all places). When you decide to seek God's intervention and miracles in your life's challenges, follow the outline in this book, put your faith in the fire of the Word of God, and pray, your miracles shall, without doubt, appear. You will not be disappointed. In Jesus' mighty name. Amen.

PRAYER 1

RECEIVING DIVINE POWER FOR GREAT EXPLOITS

BIBLE VERSE: Acts 2:3

INTRODUCTION

Simply stated, "divine power" is the "supernatural ability to do something." An "exploit" is an "extraordinary deed." Therefore, receiving divine power for great exploits means acquiring the supernatural ability to do great and extraordinary deeds. Power becomes divine when it comes from God above. He gives power by His Spirit to all who deserve it and in answer to the sincere request of the receiver.

It is very important to note here some of the truths about divine power:

1. Divine power is the most important spiritual weapon that every believer in Christ must have

2. The success or otherwise of our Christian journey depends, to a large extent, on the level of divine power we have
3. Divine power in the lives of believers enables various exploits (powerful or extraordinary deeds) to be accomplished
4. The extent to which God will use you depends on the amount of divine power possessed.

Believers in Christ, like the apostles, are essentially the ones who deserve the gift of supernatural ability to do extraordinary deeds. They are not just called out of the drowning world but are also expected to be instruments in the hands of God to rescue those who remain in the troubled and stormy rivers of life through the supernatural power received from Him (Micah 3:8). It is very sad, however, that not many believers take the time to discover or fulfil the expectation of the LORD. Instead, divine power, if actually received, is devoted to commercial or wrong purposes. The desire for flamboyant living, building edifices, and seeking earthly glories has taken the steam out of the fire in the divine power received. As a result, many have lost or operated at the lowest level of divine power.

In view of the above, it becomes expedient for a platform of prayers to be provided to address any shortcomings in our divine purpose. As you sincerely tarry before the LORD in these prayers, you shall be lifted in power to do exploits for

Him. I prophesy, therefore, that the LORD shall lay His hands on you, breathe on you, and release His cloven tongues of fire on you afresh to do great exploits for Him. In Jesus' mighty name. Amen.

PRAYER POINTS:

1. Most powerful and gracious God, I bless Your most holy name and thank You for the abundance of Your grace and power in my life. Be exalted in my life forever. In the name of Jesus.

2. I plead the blood of Jesus Christ and cover myself and all that belongs to me with the precious blood. In the name of Jesus.

3. Holy Ghost, come down with Your fire now and ignite my prayers. In the name of Jesus.

4. Blood of Jesus, break and wipe out the foundational curse or covenant that formed the basis of spiritual weakness in my life. In the name of Jesus.

5. Power that refuses to let me go and possess my divine power, I command you, by the authority of heaven, be burnt to ashes. In the name of Jesus.

6. Any power assigned to mock the power of God in my life, be disgraced by the mighty power of God. In the name of Jesus.

7. Power of God that swallows up the powers of sorcerers, diviners, and evil spiritual consultants, fall upon me now. In the name of Jesus.
8. Power of God that disgraces failures and discouragement in my life, fall upon me now. In the name of Jesus.
9. Power of God that enables one to mount up with wings as the eagle, fall upon me now. In the name of Jesus.
10. Power of God that removes tiredness from spiritual journeys, possess my life now. In the name of Jesus.
11. Power of God that confronts mountains and gets them swallowed up in the seas, come upon me now. In the name of Jesus.
12. Power of God that enables one to stand up for God to do mighty and extraordinary works, fall upon me now. In the name of Jesus.
13. Conspiracy of the dark kingdom against my divine power, prosperity, and peace, scatter by the thunder and fire of God. In Jesus' name.
14. My life and the power of God in me shall manifest the glory of God. In the name of Jesus.
15. LORD, I thank You for answering these prayers by Your fire. In the name of Jesus.

PRAYER 2

HAVE MERCY ON ME, O LORD

BIBLE VERSES: Psalm 57:1-3; Mark 10: 47-52

INTRODUCTION

One of the most valuable things in the lives of believers in Christ is "mercy." It is what makes God real in believers' lives. Without the mercy of God, it is very likely that Jesus Christ would not have come and salvation would have been impossible.

God has spoken of His plan to redeem man in Genesis 3: 15: "And I will put enmity between thee and the woman; and between thy seed and her seed; it shall bruise thy head, and thou shall bruise his heel." Therefore, at the right time, He executed His word and Christ (the seed of the woman) came. Hallelujah!

What is the mercy of God?

It is the kindness shown by God to human beings. It is something for which one needs to be grateful to God having been forgiven of deadly condemnation. It is also interpreted to mean compassion, which is to show pity.

When God created man He made him in His image. Man received the breath and nature of God. Shortly after, the image and nature got corrupted by sin and the glory bestowed on man was lost to the Devil. Therefore, everyone born of human procreation was laden with sin.

Through the power of sin from that period down to the present time, the entire human race has been engulfed in diverse problems. For example, irrespective of spiritual status – saved or not – man still:

a. Faces trials of various kinds
b. Is reproached and persecuted
c. Is hedged into bondage
d. Is fearful and faint-hearted
e. Is almost or about to give up

Through the nature and character of God, everything He does for the benefit of human beings comes from His mercy and compassion.

Illustrations of God's mercy in peoples' lives include,

a) Lot received mercy from God and was not consumed by the destruction of Sodom (Genesis 19:19)

b) David was in serious trouble, running from the evil pursuit of King Saul. Through God's mercy, he overcame (Psalm 57:1-3)

c) Blind Bartimaeus asked for and received mercy from God (Mark 10:47-52)

d) The son of the widow of Nain was restored to life through the mercy of God (Luke 7:13)

e) Zaccheus received salvation through the mercy of God (Luke 19:9-10)

Through the mercy of God demonstrated in the affairs of these people, they received uncommon deliverance from their respective problems. Through faith in God, it is possible to receive the mercy of God. As you pray now, put your faith on fire; open your heart to Him and receive a definite intervention in your situation by His mercy. In Jesus' name.

PRAYER POINTS:

1. LORD, I thank You because You are kind and Your mercies endure forever.
2. I plead the blood of Jesus for total cleansing and coverage. In the name of Jesus.
3. By Your unlimited mercy, O LORD, forgive every word or false accusation. In the name of Jesus.

4. LORD, visit me today with Your mercy, grace, and power. In the name of Jesus.

5. Make Your face to shine upon my family and me. Save us for Your mercies' sake, O LORD. In the name of Jesus.

6. God of glory and mercy, manifest Your power in my life today. In the name of Jesus.

7. Evil powers of my father's house fighting against my faith in Christ, die by fire. In the name of Jesus.

8. Spirit and power of true salvation, fall upon me now. In the name of Jesus.

9. Blood of Jesus, wash away every sin of unbelief, ignorance, and weakness in my life. In the name of Jesus.

10. Holy Spirit, fill me with living faith for my miracle. In the name of Jesus.

11. Whatever in my life makes You angry, O LORD, uproot it by Your fire. In the name of Jesus.

12. Power of the accuser of the brethren in my life, be paralyzed and disgraced. In the name of Jesus.

13. Every object of shame and disgrace in my life and family, catch fire and burn to ashes. In the name of Jesus.

14. Enemies of my success and breakthrough, receive permanent disgrace. In the name of Jesus.

15. LORD, receive all adoration and praise for answering my prayers and blessings. In the name of Jesus.

PRAYER 3

SET MY FAITH ON FIRE, O LORD

BIBLE VERSE: *2 Kings 1:10*

INTRODUCTION

Faith can be explained as believing in God's character, that is, who He is, and the confidence in God fulfilling all He has said in His Word. To have one's faith set on fire, therefore, is to attain the highest intensity of faith for spiritual exploits.

Faith is an essential factor in the relationship of human beings with God. The Bible says, "And without faith it is impossible to please God because anyone who comes to him must believe that he exists and that he rewards those who earnestly seek him" (Hebrews 11:6, NIV). A believer is one who has been redeemed from the sinful past and by the grace of God translated into the life and kingdom of the Son of God (Colossians 1:13). Whatever is done by such a believer, henceforth, must depend on the knowledge and direction of the one who now rules over the regenerated life. By the profession of faith, every action of the believer is expected to be at the disposal of God. "Many are the plans in a man's heart, but it is the LORD's purpose that prevails" (Proverbs 19:21, NIV).

In relation to the topic, it is quite appropriate to consider the reference of Jesus Christ to the ministry of John the Baptist. "From the days of John the Baptist until now, the kingdom of heaven has been forcefully advancing, and forceful men lay hold on it" (Matthew 11:12, NIV). Here, Jesus Christ was talking about the need to be violent in our faith for the kingdom business. It is most unlikely, if not impossible, for the believer and, indeed, the minister of the gospel without the faith of Elijah, to operate effectively in this present dispensation.

As a believer, there is a need to reach out unto the LORD in prayers to set your faith on fire for power and spiritual exploits. Therefore, I prophesy that the Spirit of grace shall be poured down abundantly upon you from above and your faith shall be set on fire for spiritual exploits. In Jesus' mighty name. Amen.

PRAYER POINTS:

1. Wonderful and righteous Father, I give You praise, honour, and adoration for the abundance of Your grace upon my life.

2. I confess every shortcoming that is capable of hindering my prayers. In the name of Jesus.
3. I plead the blood of Jesus Christ for total cleansing and coverage. In the name of Jesus.
4. Holy Spirit, ignite my faith with Your fire. In the name of Jesus.
5. Holy Ghost fire, delve into the foundation of my life and terminate every operation of ancestral wickedness. In the name of Jesus.
6. Holy Ghost, purge my spiritual antenna with Your fire. In the name of Jesus.
7. Powers assigned to make me powerless, be destroyed by the fire of God. In the name of Jesus.
8. Every spirit of disobedience sponsoring stubborn problems in my life, I bind you and break your power in my life. In the name of Jesus.
9. Holy Ghost fire, consume every spirit of confusion or deception in my life. In the name of Jesus.
10. Every "Jonah" assigned to scatter my journey in life, LORD, remove him from my way. In Jesus' name.
11. By Your unfailing love, O LORD, sow into my life the seed of the faith of Abraham. In the name of Jesus.
12. My God and my Father, remove me from the wrong company and position me with the people ordained for my breakthrough. In Jesus' name.

13. LORD, set the fire of my faith to the highest intensity for spiritual exploits. In the name of Jesus.
14. LORD, clothe my life with unshakable faith and fire like Elijah. In the name of Jesus.
15. LORD, I thank You for answering these prayers by Your fire. In the name of Jesus.

PRAYER 4

GOD'S MIRACLES OR BLESSINGS ARE AS LARGE AS YOUR FAITH

BIBLE VERSES: 2 Kings 4:1-6

INTRODUCTION

To believers, faith is believing that what LORD says will come to pass. In other words, it is believing God's words.

God spoke and still speaks through the Bible and His anointed servants on virtually every issue that affects man. 2 Kings Chapter 4 records four of God's miracles through the prophet Elisha:

1) Money for a poverty-stricken widow (2 Kings 4:1-7)
2) Raising a dead boy to life (2 Kings 14-37)
3) Purifying poisonous food (2 Kings 38-41)
4) Providing food for 100 men (2 Kings 42-44)

These miracles show God's tender care for those who have faith in Him.

For our illustration today, we take the poverty-stricken widow. The oil stopped pouring only when she ran out of containers. The number of containers she gathered was an indication of the strength of her faith. God's provision was as large as her faith and willingness to obey the instructions.

Beware of limiting God's blessings by your lack of faith and obedience. God is able to do immeasurably more than we can ask or imagine (Ephesians 3:20).

Here are some truths about faith:

a) Trouble comes with the lack of faith (Numbers 20:8,12)
b) Faith grows when it is exercised (Genesis 50:24)
c) Faith comes alive when we apply the scriptures (Psalm 119:125)
d) All things are possible with faith (Mark 9:23)
e) Through faith, the promises are received (Hebrews 6:12)
f) Through faith, it is possible to please God and be rewarded by Him (Hebrews 11:6)

A critical aspect of faith is that without it, it is impossible to please God, become a member of His kingdom or receive anything from Him.

For Him to act in your situation today, you must believe all He has promised to do and the testimonies of those who have received His blessings. Give yourself to Him and promise to live for Him henceforth. Make your request as big as possible and trust Him for no small miracles. He will surely surprise you. In Jesus' name.

PRAYER POINTS:

1. LORD, I thank You for Your awesome power to bless.
2. Holy Spirit, fill me with the living faith for my miracles. In the name of Jesus.
3. Holy Ghost fire, destroy all the power that anxiety and worry have over my life. In the name of Jesus.
4. Whatever is in my life that makes it difficult for my faith to grow into the right stature, Holy Ghost, uproot it by Your fire. In the name of Jesus.
5. Holy Spirit, ignite my faith with Your fire for effectiveness. In the name of Jesus.
6. Anger and sorrowful spirits robbing me of my miracles and blessings, be flushed out of my life by the fire of God. In the name of Jesus.
7. Household enemies monitoring my life for evil, receive permanent blindness. In the name of Jesus.
8. Give me the heart of obedience and belief to walk in Your way, O LORD. In the name of Jesus.

9. Spirits of fear and unbelief in my life, be destroyed by the fire of God. In the name of Jesus.

10. LORD, lift Your mighty hand against my adversaries and subdue them. In the name of Jesus.

11. Frustrate the plan and counsel of the dark kingdom against my life and family. In the name of Jesus.

12. LORD, anywhere my life and blessings are being held hostage, command Your angel Michael to liberate them. In the name of Jesus.

13. Mountain of disappointment, hear the Word of the LORD. Move out of my life and be cast into the sea. In the name of Jesus.

14. My faith, refuse to be limited by weakness and carelessness but rise up for your miracles. In the name of Jesus.

15. By the power and authority of heaven, my vessels of blessings shall not dry. In the name of Jesus.

PRAYER 5

TEACH MY HANDS TO WAR AND MY FINGERS TO FIGHT, O LORD!

BIBLE VERSE: Psalm 144:1

INTRODUCTION

The statement "Teach my hands to war and my fingers to fight" is a figurative one. It is designed to express the help needed and the actions to be taken to be effective in warfare. When applied to spiritual warfare, it simply means what is required to become effective in warfare prayers.

The psalmist's choice of words in our Bible verse for today came from his perception of the LORD's supernatural role that brought him extraordinary success in his battles. Even though we know that God is a Spirit (John 4:24 a) and He cannot be seen physically, His presence in the affairs and outcomes of believers' actions is without a doubt (Proverbs 16:1; 19:21). By His Spirit, the heart of man is instructed about the strategy to be used in such actions and directed to the kind of results intended by the LORD (Proverbs 21:1).

As believers in Christ, understanding the truth of the LORD's awesome power and knowledge (omnipotence and omniscience) should allow Him to teach us His pattern in a battle that ensures victory. This is the secret the psalmist discovered and took advantage of very well. This understanding also informed the focus of these prayers in which we seek more instruction from the LORD to be effective in our battles. I prophesy, therefore, that the LORD shall be entreated by your prayers to teach and perfect your hand and fingers in all your battles. He shall give you victory like the psalmist. In Jesus' mighty name. Amen.

PRAYER POINTS:

1. Invisible and Most High God, I worship You and bless Your most holy name for Your faithfulness in my life and family. Receive all praise and adoration forever. In the name of Jesus.

2. I plead the blood of Jesus for cleansing and coverage. In the name of Jesus.

3. Holy Ghost power and fire, fall upon me now. In the name of Jesus.

4. Spirit of grace and might, fall upon me now. In the name of Jesus.

5. I break and loose myself from every evil curse of limitation. In the name of Jesus.
6. Holy Ghost fire, purge every form of lukewarmness in my life and prayers. In the name of Jesus.
7. Every weapon that the enemies are relying upon to fight me and my family, LORD, render them impotent and useless in their hands. In the name of Jesus.
8. Rock of Ages, grind into powder every occult priest, altar or instrument assigned to divert the course of Your blessings for my life and family. In the name of Jesus.
9. LORD, expose and nullify by the blood of Jesus every form of demonic manipulation in my life or contact with their agents. In the name of Jesus.
10. Holy Spirit, nourish me continually in the Word and power of God. In the name of Jesus.
11. In all the battles that I need to fight, LORD, teach me to be effective and lead me to victory. In the name of Jesus.
12. My Father, my Maker, lift up my hand upon my adversaries and cause them to be cut off. In the name of Jesus.
13. I refuse to faint in the day of adversity but to consider You, LORD, as my strength. In the name of Jesus.

14. LORD, keep me strong and courageous in all my assignments before You. In the name of Jesus.
15. Faithful LORD, I thank You for answering these prayers promptly and by Your fire. In the name of Jesus.

PRAYER 6

PREVAILING IN BATTLES

BIBLE VERSES: Psalm 18:37-46

INTRODUCTION

A "battle" is "a lengthy and difficult conflict or struggle," while "to prevail" is "to prove more powerful or superior." Hence, "prevailing in battles" means "to prove more powerful or superior in any conflict or struggle." Battles are generally fought in the physical between two opposing forces. Battles that are spiritual also exist in the sense that they cannot be seen physically. Spiritual battles, like any other battles, are struggles between two or more contending parties. In other words, they are between the oppressed (human victims) and the oppressor (enemies under satanic control).

Spiritual battles are not fought in the same way as physical battles because spiritual battles are not seen physically. Much as spiritual battles are not seen or fought in the physical so also are the weapons used.

> For the weapons of our warfare are not carnal but mighty in God for pulling down strongholds, casting down arguments and every high thing that exalts itself against the knowledge of God, bringing every thought into captivity to the obedience of Christ. (2 Corinthians 10:4,5, NKJV)

Our Christian journey (life) is fraught (filled) with battles. If in doubt, ask our forefather David. However, while David's battles were to a large extent physical, most, if not all Christians' (believers') battles are spiritual. The essence of our Christian experience includes our ability to live above every form of oppression. To be victorious, that is, to prevail over oppressors, believers will definitely fight battles using their authority and weapons from heaven. This is so because the enemies of believers are the Devil, his demons (fallen angels), and all human agents. These enemies headed by the Devil have as their duty "to steal, and to kill, and to destroy" (John 10:10).

As we pray these prayers using spiritual weapons and with the LORD Jesus Christ on our side as the commander of the hosts of heaven, we shall surely prevail. Therefore, I prophesy that the LORD shall hear your prayers, fight on your behalf, and give you the power and strength to prevail in all your battles. In Jesus' mighty name. Amen.

PRAYER POINTS:

1. Heavenly Father, I bless and worship You for being my rock, fortress, strength, and deliverer.
2. I plead the blood of Jesus Christ for cleansing of shortcomings and total coverage. In the name of Jesus.
3. Blood of Jesus Christ, break and destroy every curse of failure in my life. In the name of Jesus.
4. LORD, in this battle, teach my hands to war and my fingers to fight. In the name of Jesus.
5. Holy Spirit, ignite my life, faith, and prayers with Your fire for effectiveness. In the name of Jesus.
6. Release Your warfare angels for my sake with instruction to pursue my stubborn enemies to destruction. In the name of Jesus.
7. Make the weapons and plans of my enemies useless in their hands, O LORD. In the name of Jesus.
8. Holy Ghost, dismantle and destroy the platform my enemies are standing on to fight me. In the name of Jesus.
9. Holy Ghost, break the jaws of godless oppressors in my life with Your thunder. In the name of Jesus.
10. According to Your Word in Psalm 63:9, O LORD, I command those seeking my soul to destroy it, to die their own death. In the name of Jesus.

11. Powers that have turned my life into recurring battles, be roasted by the fire of God, In the name of Jesus.
12. I receive the sword of fire and slaughter every satanic animal tormenting my dreams. In Jesus' name.
13. All warfare prepared against my peace and progress, receive divine destruction. In the name of Jesus.
14. With the strength of God, I subdue and prevail over those who rose against me. In the name of Jesus.
15. LORD Jesus, I thank You for answers and the miracles that will follow. In Jesus' name.

PRAYER 7

LOOK UP, HELP IS COMING.

BIBLE VERSES: *Psalm 121:1-4*

INTRODUCTION

Faith is a very important aspect of human life and for believers (Christians). It is not only important, but it is also a powerful instrument of success on the journey of life.

Those who do not have or value faith may not be able to leave home, allow their children to go to school and come back or even venture into any kind of work or business.

For the believer, the tool of faith is powerful. To draw from the miracles, which are supernatural works of God in the lives of His people, we must have it. The prayer focus of today, "Look up. Help is coming" is the message to you from the LORD, the miracle worker Himself. Because He knows the situations and needs of everyone, He is more than able to address them and meet those needs.

Some people are worried about where and when the help will come for them to pay their children's school fees or buy their books and uniforms. Some people are in debt, while others have money tied up in one way or the other. Some people are battling with one sickness or the other; they are tired of telling people about their sufferings. They may have been prayed for time and time again without any breakthrough. Hear the words of the LORD, "Fear not" (Isaiah 41:10).

Let us look briefly at some illustrations in the Bible:

- Help for Hagar (Genesis 21:14-19)
- Provision for Abraham (Genesis 22:13)
- Help to Samson (Judges 16:28-30)
- Help for Jeremiah (Jeremiah 40:5)
- Healing for the woman with the issue of blood (Mark 5:25-34)
- Help for the widow of Nain, etc. (Luke 7:13-16)

In this kind of prayer programme, everything is done by faith. Even though no miracle can be done by common sense, the miracle worker Himself, Jesus Christ is well known. The assignment here is to link you with Him. Hear Him again,

> And call upon me in the day of trouble: I will deliver thee, and thou shalt glorify me. (Psalm 50:15)

With His Spirit present, God is saying to you although your needs may be many and as urgent and serious as those of the people of Jabesh-Gilead in 1 Samuel 11, fear not because your help is on the way!

As you begin to pray, remember to put your faith to work by surrendering your entire life to Jesus Christ. Promise to continue living for Him and claim your miracles.

PRAYER POINTS:

1. Ever faithful God, I bless Your most holy name for Your kindness and mercies that endure forever.
2. Blood of Jesus cleanse me and remove every curse of limitation in my life. In the name of Jesus.
3. Every spirit of fear tormenting my life be uprooted by the fire of God. In the name of Jesus.
4. Doors of disappointment that fear opened for my life, be closed permanently. In the name of Jesus.
5. Powers pushing me back into the world for help, be disgraced out of my life. In the name of Jesus.
6. God, arise in my situation now and make every impossibility possible. In the name of Jesus.
7. God my present help in trouble, appear in my situation now and send down the rain of your help into my life. Silence all the mouths of the wicked. In the name of Jesus.

8. LORD, dry up the source of poverty in my life and open the gates of goodness unto me. In the name of Jesus.

9. Any power sitting on my divine blessing, be unseated and die by the fire of God. In the name of Jesus.

10. The LORD who makes a way through the sea and a path through the mighty waters shall make a way for me. In the name of Jesus.

11. Open unto me and my family Your rivers of blessings and breakthrough, O LORD. In the name f Jesus.

12. LORD, grant me the power to wait and be patient with You in all my requests. In the name of Jesus.

13. The LORD shall take me out of Lo-debar and move me into my palace today. In the name of Jesus.

14. On my Christian journey, I shall no longer be tired or discouraged. In the name of Jesus.

15. LORD, I thank You for the prompt answer and testimony that shall follow. In the name of Jesus.

PRAYER 8

COURAGE IN TROUBLED TIMES

BIBLE VERSES: 2 Chronicles 15:3-15

INTRODUCTION

- Troubled times are periods beset by problems or difficulties when things are not in their expected condition. They are not pleasant times at all. Any Christian (believer) who has experienced war, serious illness, loss of loved ones, extreme poverty, calamities or faced death, knows this very well. Even King Asa of Judah and all Israel had their troubled times (2 Chronicles 15:5-6).
- Troubled times are not desirable or expected but their possibility is very high. Even the Word of God says, "In the last days perilous times shall come" (2 Timothy 3:1). We are already in the last days. We know this by the strange things that are happening in the world.

- When troubled times come, life becomes miserable suggesting that something has gone wrong in the spiritual realm and is now manifesting in the physical realm. Despite extensive prayers, they may still appear and persist. It seems as if God is not hearing those prayers. The Word of God asks us to be courageous (Joshua 1:9), to be strong in the spirit and fearless.
- In the case of King Asa and Judah, they heard the Word of God and showed great courage and love for God. Because of their obedience, they were given peace and rest from troubles (2 Corinthians 15:15).
- Some lessons to be learnt about troubled times are:
  a) Useful in their abilities to prune us (2 Corinthians 4:15).
  b) Show who you really are – the kind of character you have developed
  c) Help you recognize the need for God and develop faith to make it grow stronger
  d) Help you to move closer to God and draw from His promises
  e) Enable the glory and power of God to be exhibited when we overcome and testify.

- Therefore, in troubled times, do not complain or murmur against God about your situations. Rather, pray to God about them and wait for His intervention. The trouble you face today is training you to be strong and courageous for more challenging situations in the future, which we must pray against now. Finally, God's ultimate plan to allow you to go through troubled times is to bring you out as gold (Job 23:10).
- Before you pray, make sure that Jesus Christ is in full control of your life. As one of His children, your deliverance from troubled times shall glorify Him. In Jesus' mighty name. Amen.

PRAYER POINTS:

1. Covenant keeping God, I bless You and honour Your most holy name for Your power to deliver.
2. I plead the blood of Jesus Christ for my cleansing and coverage. In the name of Jesus.
3. Any trouble that came into my life as a result of ignorance, in Your mercy, O LORD, cancel it. In the name of Jesus.
4. Every seed of the Devil in my life and family, Holy Ghost, uproot it. In the name of Jesus.

5. Foundational curse from my father and mother's house crying for fulfilment, be broken and nullified by the blood of Jesus. In Jesus' name.

6. Any trouble that came from my act of helping or supporting others, LORD, fight for me and deliver me. In the name of Jesus.

7. Blood of Jesus, break and nullify every covenant of trouble and suffering entered or made against my life and family. In the name of Jesus.

8. LORD, silence all the rage and rampage of the Devil and his wicked agents in my life and family. In the name of Jesus.

9. God, arise and bring into judgment all the disobedience of environmental powers to Your authority, given for my deliverance. In the name of Jesus.

10. I reject all the counsel of the Enemy to go through life with his compass. In the name of Jesus.

11. LORD, be my strength and build up my courage in troubled times. In the name of Jesus.

12. In any test You allow me to go through, O LORD, bring me out as gold. In the name of Jesus.

13. In troubled times, let Your mercy and truth continually preserve me, O LORD. In the name of Jesus.

14. I refuse to live a wasted life but resolve to walk with the LORD to finish well. In the name of Jesus.
15. Good tidings of great joy shall fall upon me as a result of my prayers today. In the name of Jesus.

PRAYER 9

THERE IS HOPE FOR YOU (YOU ARE NOT HOPELESS)

BIBLE VERSES: Job 14:7-9; 1 Peter 1:3-5

INTRODUCTION

- Hope is the expectation of the fulfilment of something desired or promised. Hope is one of the three pillars of faith, hope, and trust that are required for believers' supernatural blessings.
- While faith is to believe, trust is to be confident. Believers are expected to believe all the promises of God. But despite this fact, some believers are caught up in the web of despair, suicide bids or really committing the same.
- Job's view in Job14:14 was limited to the natural perception of the resurrection of the dead, which he held in probability while that of the plant was considered real and feasible (Job 7-9). Our hope even of the resurrection of the dead is based on

Christ's promise (John 11:25). We now know that the dead will rise since Jesus Christ Himself arose. Hence, our hope of resurrection is sure (2 Peter 1:13-14).

- By the Word of God, believers have hope in the following other areas:
  - Hope of salvation (Romans 8:24)
  - Hope of an antidote for despair (Jeremiah 31:17)
  - Hope of our inheritance (Ephesians 1:18)
  - Hope of a calling (Colossians 1:27)
  - Blessed hope (Titus 2:13)
  - Hope of an anchor (Hebrews 6:19)
- Our God is faithful, His mercies are new every morning and evening; therefore, nothing should trouble the hearts of believers because their Father loves His children and cannot forsake them (Lamentations 3:21; John 14:1; Hebrews 13:5).
- Whatever your needs or what you may be passing through, God is saying, "There is hope for you in areas of provision, healing, deliverance, favour, prosperity, protection, and peace." Give your life to Him totally and call upon Him for what you need. Make your hope in God an antidote for any despair and an anchor for your soul. Have confidence in

what He says concerning you. It will surely come to pass. Therefore, I prophesy that since He who made the promise is faithful, He will appear in your situation now and meet your needs. In Jesus' mighty name. Amen.

PRAYER POINTS:

1. Everlasting Father, I bless and honour Your holy name because You are the hope of the hopeless.
2. I plead the blood of Jesus Christ for cleansing and total coverage. In the name of Jesus.
3. Holy Spirit, ignite my faith with Your fire. In the name of Jesus.
4. Blood of Jesus, cancel all negative effects of ignorance in my life. In the name of Jesus.
5. Powers assigned to rob me of God's mercy and grace, be exposed and destroyed by the fire of God. In the name of Jesus.
6. Holy Ghost fire, burn to ashes every coven of witchcraft in my environment. In the name of Jesus.
7. Conspiracy of the dark kingdom against my faith, hope, and trust in the promises of God for my life, be scattered by the thunder and fire of God. In the name of Jesus.

8. Unseen powers using evil hands to trouble my life and destiny, be exposed and destroyed by the fire of God. In the name of Jesus.

9. LORD, cast out of my life the wicked and all evil counsellors in the multitude of their transgressions. In the name of Jesus.

10. Holy Ghost, break open any satanic strong room holding my spiritual and physical provisions, so I can receive them. In the name of Jesus.

11. LORD, overturn and consume by Your fire every demonic throne of judgment set up to kill my living hope in God. In the name of Jesus.

12. Holy Ghost fire and blood of Jesus, purify my thoughts for the living hope in God to thrive in my heart. In the name of Jesus.

13. LORD, let me not be ashamed of my hope in You and Your promises for my life. In the name of Jesus.

14. By Your supernatural operation in my life, restore unto me all the enemies deceitfully took away from my family and me. In the name of Jesus.

15. LORD, I thank You for Your answer to these prayers and renewing my hope in You. In the name of Jesus.

PRAYER 10

DO NOT GIVE UP ON ME. WAKE UP MY HELPERS TO HELP ME, O LORD

BIBLE VERSES: *Luke 11:5-10; Esther 6:1-10*

INTRODUCTION

Bad reports such as calamities, disasters, epidemics, terrorism, kidnappings, and unpleasant occurrences have taken over the news on a regular basis. Whenever we hear such news and reports we tend to believe them even when they are false. Such beliefs keep us in fear and anxiety. These situations also give rise to serious doubt about whether God is in control of the affairs of the world.

It is painful to find that many so-called believers are caught up in the same web of fear and worry. While it is possible for believers to experience the same unpleasant situations as unbelievers in the world such as war, epidemics, famine and insecurity (Job 5:6-7), it is very important that believers' reactions to unpleasant situations are completely different.

Knowledge of the Word of God, obedience, faith, and trust in the LORD should enable believers to make a great difference. In Luke 11:5-10, Jesus Christ speaks about the need to continue asking for God's intervention in our affairs. Esther 6:1-10 shows that God is always in control and at work in the affairs of His people. He will not give up on us or allow our helper to sleep until our blessings are released to us (Deuteronomy 31:6; Jeremiah 29:12-13).

To enable God to rise and act in your situation, you must be a believer. When you surrender your life to Jesus Christ, it becomes easy for Him to be your refuge and fortress and act in your situation.

What is that problem in your life? Is it poverty, sickness, fear of evil or untimely death, worry and anxiety, failure, delay, rejection, dejection, reproach or persecution that refuses to go away? Today, the divine helper will arise and cause the channel of your breakthrough to open and flow into you. In Jesus' mighty name. Amen.

PRAYER POINTS:

1. Helper of the helpless, I bless and honour Your name for Your great providence on me and my family.
2. Whatever came through the eye, ear, nose, mouth, and brought fear and anxiety into my life, blood of

Jesus and fire of God, destroy them. In the name of Jesus.

3. Powers of household enemies assigned to monitor my life for limitation and stagnation, Holy Ghost Fire, consume them. In the name of Jesus.

4. Thunder of God, scatter every conspiracy of the dark kingdom to lay siege against my life and family. In the name of Jesus.

5. Arrows of evil words fired into my life and destiny, come out of my life; return to sender and backfire. In the name of Jesus.

6. Blood of Jesus, flush out all the evil food eaten in the dream and designed to poison me. In the name of Jesus.

7. Lion of Judah, chase out affliction, suffering, and bondage from my life and family. In the name of Jesus.

8. Blood of Jesus, wipe out every record of failure from my endeavours. In the name of Jesus.

9. LORD, unseat any power sitting upon or hiding the records of my success. Release and announce them. In the name of Jesus.

10. I withdraw my finances from the hands of familiar spirits and all dead relatives. In the name of Jesus.

11. Whatsoever has been hindering my progress physically and spiritually, give way now. In the name of Jesus.
12. Any power or human being holding my glory illegally or trading with it, LORD, cause it to be returned by fire. In the name of Jesus.
13. Do not give up on me, O LORD but let Your help compass me about. In the name of Jesus.
14. Divine Helper, arise in Your power and wake up all my helpers for their assignment concerning me. In the name of Jesus.
15. Glory and peace of God for my life and family, arise, shine, and never grow dim again. In the name of Jesus.

PRAYER 11

SHOW AND LEAD ME IN THE RIGHT WAY, O LORD

BIBLE VERSES: *Psalm 25:8-10; 32:8; Isaiah 30:21*

INTRODUCTION

Parents have the responsibility of bringing up their children and providing them with everything they need in life. They are to guide them in the right way, so they will grow up properly. As soon as children mature and can stand for themselves, they should follow the right way in terms of employment opportunities and marriage. The right or wrong choice in these two areas will eventually determine their success or failure.

The major problem with human beings is our desire to pattern our lives on each other, instead of the LORD. For example,

1. Choosing names for our children. A name may be beautiful to call, but it may not glorify the LORD. An example of such a name is one which means

"father or mother has come back." This is a common name in some African societies. However, when a father or mother who had nothing worthy of remembrance comes back through the life of the child, what good is it?

2. The choice of a child's profession – desire to be a doctor when the child ought to be an engineer.
3. The choice of the person to marry or desire to marry someone rich only to discover the person is deeply involved in the occult or witchcraft, etc.

More often than not, all efforts made in the above instances lead to failure, disappointment, and frustration. However, when a parent or a person is aware of the importance of God's direction in every aspect of life, God will most likely be actively involved and the desired success is guaranteed (Psalm 18:30; 32:8).

Without wasting much time, this prayer assignment is the opportunity to confess every form of disobedience, seek God's mercy in humility and for Him to show and lead us into His way. He will be merciful to us and send His favour with the blessings for holding on to His way.

PRAYER POINTS:

1. Ever faithful God, I praise and honour You for Your presence in my life and situation.

2. Holy Ghost fire, uproot every spirit of error and absent-mindedness planted in my life by familiar spirits. In the name of Jesus.

3. Holy Ghost thunder, break into pieces every satanic compass of my father's house, dictating my way in life. In the name of Jesus.

4. Holy Ghost, dismantle every roadblock and checkpoint of environmental powers in my life. In the name of Jesus.

5. LORD, in Your mercy and power, reverse every wrong way I have taken or led anyone. In the name of Jesus.

6. Blood of Jesus, nullify every negative outcome of the wrong way already taken in my life. In the name of Jesus.

7. Whatever has been standing against my success and breakthrough in any area of my life, LORD, dismantle now. In the name of Jesus.

8. LORD, arrange my life and destiny in line with Your original plan. In the name of Jesus.

9. LORD, by Your mercy, restore all the good things, positions, blessings, and rewards that were missed because I followed my own way. In the name of Jesus.

10. Show me thy way and teach me thy path. In the name of Jesus.

11. By Your Spirit, O LORD, lead and guide me and my family in Your way. In the name of Jesus.
12. LORD, frustrate satanic deceits and manipulations in my life. In the name of Jesus.
13. LORD, by Your Spirit, equip me to be fully dependable. In the name of Jesus.
14. From now, I shall not walk in circles but in the right direction of the Holy Spirit. In the name of Jesus.
15. LORD, receive all adoration for Your prompt answer to my prayers. In the name of Jesus.

PRAYER 12

OPEN MY EYES TO SEE YOUR WELL OF BLESSINGS, O LORD

BIBLE VERSES: Genesis 21:14 – 19

INTRODUCTION

The most important thing in the life of a believer after being born again is the difficulty to change from the previous Adamic nature into Christlikeness and righteousness (2 Corinthians 5:17; Ephesians 4:24).

As apostle Paul put it clearly in Galatians 5:17, the flesh (Adamic nature) "lusteth against the Spirit" to make it difficult for good things to happen in the life of the believer.

The background story of Hagar, Sarah's handmaid, reveals that Hagar boldly mocked Sarah, her mistress through pride; this displeased Sarah. It is very clear that the wealth of Abraham could sustain the two of them as wives if Hagar had humbled herself. Eventually, Hagar and her son were sent away to wander in the wilderness of Beer-sheba. Hagar became miserable when her provision was spent and there was no more water for her child. All she could do was cry. She thought she and the child would die. But the LORD opened her eyes, and she saw a well of water that sustained her (Genesis 21:19).

Many believers are in the same position as Hagar; hence, lots of troubles come upon them, which are capable of changing their lives negatively, for example, Gideon, Jephthah, and Samson in the book of Judges).

The all-sufficient God is merciful, and His power is infinitely greater than any other. He knows every bit of your situation and is more than able to meet every need of His children. Also, it makes good sense to rely on Him for uncommon blessings. Call upon Him now (Psalm 50:15). Ask Him now (Matthew 7:7). His answer is just a call away!

Before you pray, you must ensure you have a right relationship with Jesus Christ and by faith live for Him. When you cry unto the LORD in prayer now, be assured He will hear you and open your eyes to your miracles of blessings.

PRAYER POINTS:

1. All-sufficient God, I worship You for Your ability to meet all my needs today.
2. Holy Ghost, ignite my faith and prayers with Your fire. In the name of Jesus.

3. Holy Ghost fire, consume every spirit of pride and stubbornness in my life. In the name of Jesus.

4. Holy Spirit, chase every inherited trait and behavior out of my life that is not pleasing to You. In the name of Jesus.

5. LORD, destroy every legal ground on which the Enemy is standing to attack my life. In the name of Jesus.

6. Holy Spirit, frustrate every evil exchange of my virtues by familiar spirits. In the name of Jesus.

7. LORD, render useless every weapon of the enemies designed to waste my life. In the name of Jesus.

8. Holy Ghost, break down the house of bondage prepared for me and my family. In the name of Jesus.

9. LORD, tear off every satanic veil blocking my eyes from beholding your blessings for my life. In the name of Jesus.

10. Any organ of my body now on the altar of darkness to cause terminal sickness, Holy Ghost, withdraw it by Your fire. In the name of Jesus.

11. LORD, open my eyes now to see and draw from Your well of blessings. In the name of Jesus.

12. God, arise and release the abundance of Your mercy and favour into my life. In the name of Jesus.

13. I recover the covenant of long life stolen from my life by ancestral powers. In the name of Jesus.

14. I shall never wander away from Your covenant of prosperity, O LORD. In the name of Jesus.
15. LORD, I thank You for answering my prayers. In the name of Jesus.

PRAYER 13

FORGET THE PAST AND PREPARE FOR NEW THINGS

BIBLE VERSES: Isaiah 43:15-21

INTRODUCTION

Human beings love to dwell on or celebrate their problems and afflictions for long periods of time. They often talk about my sickness, my mistake, my failure, my disappointment, my suffering, my trouble, etc. They repeat these words every time and often as if they have become permanent properties.

Children of God (believers in Christ) are expected to see their problems or afflictions as temporary occurrences or stopgaps. Unfortunately, the way they treat their challenging periods is not much different from the way unbelievers do.

From the time of the fall of man in the garden of Eden, God continued to remind every human being, especially those who choose to listen to Him, to have faith and trust in Him for deliverance during times of trouble or affliction. For example, Psalm 50:15; 23:4; Isaiah 43:2; 49:25, and Hebrews 13:5 are clear indications of the intention of God to deliver. When God acted on His Word and delivered, unfortunately, little time was given to praise Him. Psalm 92:12 wants us to take the sacrifice of praise unto the LORD very seriously.

Many times in the past, God spoke, and He still speaks at the present time.

> Remember ye not the former things, neither consider the things of old. Behold, I will do a new thing; now it shall spring forth; shall ye not know it? I will even make a way in the wilderness and rivers in the desert. (Isaiah 43:18, 19)

Above is a strong, ageless promise of God. He cannot deny Himself or go back on His Word. Believe this promise of God and apply it in faith to your situation and circumstances. You will see the manifestation of the power of God and new things begin to happen. God has done it many times through the name of Jesus Christ. It is written, "Jesus Christ the same yesterday and to day and forever" (Hebrews 13:8).

As you pray, remember being a true child of God having the nature of Jesus Christ and living to please Him will make your miracles appear in full.

PRAYER POINTS:

1. Covenant-keeping God, I worship You and praise Your most holy name today.

2. I plead the blood of Jesus and ask for mercy for all unbelief in my life. In the name of Jesus.

3. Holy Ghost, renew me and ignite my faith with Your fire now. In the name of Jesus.

4. Foundational powers working to confuse me and make me murmur against God, be destroyed by the fire of God. In the name of Jesus.

5. Draw me not away with the wicked and the workers of iniquity, O LORD. In the name of Jesus.

6. LORD, any part of my life drawn into satanic bondage due to ignorance and carelessness, by Your mercy, pull me out. In the name of Jesus.

7. Holy Ghost, uproot every seed of sickness, poverty, and unfruitfulness in my life and family. In the name of Jesus.

8. Rivers of affliction, reproach, and regret in my life and family, dry up from the source. In the name of Jesus.

9. Spirits of delay and disappointment in my life, die out by the fire of God. In the name of Jesus.

10. LORD, lead me and my family out of the wilderness of life and into the river of Your pleasure. In the name of Jesus.
11. The LORD shall make me and my family forget the past and begin new things in our lives. In the name of Jesus.
12. The LORD shall make the time of my success, victory, and joy permanent. In the name of Jesus.
13. The object of Your praise in my mouth shall be wonderful to silence my adversaries forever. In the name of Jesus.
14. The LORD shall bless and beautify my life and family to bring others to Him. In the name of Jesus.
15. LORD, I thank You for a prompt answer to my prayers and the miracles that will follow. In the name of Jesus.

PRAYER 14

FLESH IN MY LIFE MUST DIE

BIBLE VERSES: *1 Kings 11:1-4; Acts 5:1- 6*

INTRODUCTION

- "Flesh" in the physical realm is that part of the body other than blood, bones, veins, and water. But in the spiritual realm "flesh" represents carnality, the part of human emotions that work against the Spirit. It is that part of human beings that has fallen and refused to be revived. This statement requires further explanation.
- Genesis 1:31 tells us that everything God made at creation including human beings was good.
- Romans 5:12 also tells us that Adam and Eve (the first people on the earth) sinned and by their actions, sin entered the world. Consequently, death came because of sin. Through the love of God (John 3:16), Jesus Christ came into the world to redeem

human beings from the curse and sentence of death brought by sin.
- Thus, anyone who sincerely repents and is redeemed is expected to become a new creature (2 Corinthians 5:17). Despite the newness, the flesh continues to war against everything. In human beings, it wars especially against the spirit (Galatians 5:16-17). The manifestation of the work of the flesh can be seen in the thoughts and actions of human beings. Hence, the Bible describes the flesh as disobedient, stubborn, rebellious, and a bastard (Deuteronomy 21:18), to mention a few.
- The Bible also gives many illustrations of the impact of the flesh in the lives of people:
  a. Samson (Judges 16:15-20)
  b. Solomon (1 Kings 11:1-4)
  c. Ananias (Acts 5:1-5)
  d. Backsliding believers (Galatians 5:16)

The impact of the "flesh" in our lives is so dire we must kill it (Colossians 3:5).

- When we look at our lives critically, it is possible for us to see what the evil flesh has done or is capable of doing. When you see strange things happening in your life or that of anybody, know it is the product of the flesh (the fallen nature).

- Despite your strong faith, you still have weak points, which the Devil can exploit. He knows this very well. Hence, he will always attack you through evil thoughts and actions, which, in turn, will offend God and rob you of your blessings.
- Believers – or anyone for that matter – must be ready to put the flesh to death; otherwise, salvation stands the risk of failure. If Solomon, the wisest man on earth at the time could not subdue his flesh, it is a very serious matter. For the flesh to die in your life, you must:
  a) Be born again, that is, hear the Word of God, believe, and follow Jesus Christ
  b) Be transformed in the mind, that is, your thoughts, desires, and actions
  c) Be humble, diligent, holy, and righteous
  d) Be watchful and pray aggressively. As you begin to pray now, I prophesy that everything, which represents the flesh in your life shall be exposed, uprooted, destroyed, and expired. In Jesus' mighty name. Amen.

PRAYER POINTS:

1. Eternal Rock of Ages, I worship and praise You for Your awesome power to save and deliver.
2. I plead the blood of Jesus for total cleansing and coverage. In the name of Jesus.
3. LORD, in Your mercy, forgive every chance given to the flesh in my life. In the name of Jesus.
4. Ancestral powers assigned to sustain the work of the flesh in my life, die by the fire of God. In the name of Jesus.
5. Holy Ghost, destroy every satanic deceit that empowered the flesh in my life. In the name of Jesus.
6. Blood of Jesus, flush out every demonic contamination of food in my dream. In the name of Jesus.
7. Evil hands of poverty, wretchedness, and lack in my life, wither and burn to ashes. In the name of Jesus.
8. Every trace and control of the flesh in my life, be wiped out by the blood of Jesus. In Jesus' name.
9. Holy Ghost, paralyze the efforts of the flesh to tamper with Your plan for my life. In the name of Jesus.
10. Spirits of pride, anger, and annoyance feeding the flesh in my life, die by fire. In the name of Jesus.

11. Power and work of the flesh holding down my life and destiny, expire by fire. In the name of Jesus.

12. Holy Ghost fire, destroy every power of the wicked to cause pain in my life. In the name of Jesus.

13. LORD, lay Your hands of power, success, and prosperity upon me now. In the name of Jesus.

14. The LORD shall break the power of the flesh in my life and subdue it forever. In the name of Jesus.

15. LORD, I thank You for answering my prayers by Your fire. In the name of Jesus.

PRAYER 15

TOUCH ME WITH YOUR HEALING HAND, O LORD

BIBLE VERSES: Psalm 33:13-22; Mark 6:53-56

INTRODUCTION

- Healing is the process of making or becoming sound or healthy again. Healing and deliverance were referred to by Jesus Christ as the children's (of the kingdom) bread (Mark 7:27) and His ministry was full of healing miracles (Acts 10:38).
- The Bible verses above clearly introduce us to the Great Healer who does the work of healing among the children of men – the LORD Jesus Christ. The psalmist in Psalm 33:13-22 knew the LORD intimately from the experiences in his life. He had confidence in the LORD and testified of His ability and greatness. Mark 6:53-56 captured an event during the earthly ministry of Jesus Christ. We see the people of Gennesaret recognizing the presence

of Jesus Christ in their area, and they positioned themselves for His touch of healing and deliverance.

- Our healing and deliverance are not just being done now, they were already accomplished by the LORD's work on the cross at Calvary (Isaiah 53:5; 1 Peter 2:24; John 19:30). Jesus Christ died on the cross, rose from the dead by the power of the resurrection and is alive forevermore. Praise the LORD!

- You may be passing through (a) spiritual poverty, that is, not yet having Jesus in your life or not allowing Him to work in you (b) financial poverty, that is, causing shame and disgrace (c) sickness or infirmity that refuses to go away (d) demonic attack or oppression in bad dreams (e) failure, barrenness or unfruitfulness even at the edge of breakthroughs. Nevertheless, the Great Healer is present where you are now.

- First, recognize the presence of the great healer and deliverer close to you. Second, surrender yourself to Him, so He can touch, save, heal, deliver, and bless you. This happens when we pray.

- Third, receive your desired miracle by faith and glorify the Great Healer. You will not be disappointed. In Jesus' mighty name.

PRAYER POINTS:

1. Great Healer, I thank You and praise Your holy name for Your mighty power to heal and deliver.
2. I plead the blood of Jesus to cleanse, cover, and set me free now. In the name of Jesus.
3. LORD, I surrender my life to you. Take it over and sanitize it with Your blood. In the name of Jesus.
4. Powers waging war against my health, be destroyed by fire. In the name of Jesus.
5. Marine powers waging war against my finances, die by the fire of God. In the name of Jesus.
6. Holy Ghost, consume every demonic attacker in my dream with Your fire. In the name of Jesus.
7. Seeds of failure and unfruitfulness in my life and family, be uprooted by the fire of God. In Jesus' name.
8. LORD, cause every evil hand of sickness, infirmity, and untimely death in my life to dry up by Your fire. In the name of Jesus.
9. LORD, wipe out the effects of costly errors leading to spiritual defeat. In the name of Jesus.
10. Holy Ghost fire, uproot and burn every disease-carrying parasite hiding in my body. In the name of Jesus.

11. Any stronghold standing against my healing and deliverance, be pulled down. In the name of Jesus.
12. LORD, stretch Your hand and touch me now to accomplish the healing required. In the name of Jesus.
13. Spiritual insight, divine revelation, and discernment, come upon my life now. In the name of Jesus.
14. I shall not miss the time and season of my divine visitation. In the name of Jesus.
15. LORD, I thank You for answering my prayers and for the release of the healing virtue. In the name of Jesus.

PRAYER 16

FIX THE POTHOLES OF MY LIFE, O LORD

BIBLE VERSES: *Jeremiah 18:1-6*

INTRODUCTION

- The "potter" is one who works with clay to make different kinds of vessels. Our Bible verse (Jeremiah 18:6) shows the LORD as the "Potter" in His relationship with human beings. "Potholes" are ponds formed on the road by erosion or water making passage through the road difficult.
- Life is a journey. Physical journeys are made on the roads; this makes them liable to develop potholes by effluxion thereby making a smooth journey difficult. The "potholes" on the journey of life represent scars from bad relationships, wrong decisions, and mistakes of the past, which are hurting terribly in the present.

- The main source of people's problems is the Devil and his agents. When their works in the lives of human beings are manifested, they leave scars, which make human vessels (bodies) unacceptable. These potholes cause every journey to be very rough. When we find ourselves in these unpleasant situations, we must go to the Potter's house – the work-room of the Holy Ghost, for Him to fix the vessel.
- The "Potter" (v.6) can make a brand new vessel with our lives out of the mess. He has done it many times before:
  a) Joseph in the hands of household enemies
  b) Ruth and the family curse
  c) Hannah and the hand of God in her life
  d) The widow of Nain and the circumstances of life
  e) Children who became witches in school through initiation and tormented their parents.
- God has the power over human lives. He created them and continues to work with them to make useful vessels. However, we need to repent and turn from the co-operation given to the architect of potholes (the Devil) in human lives.

- As the Potter works on fixing our "potholes," we must not become mindless and passive – one aspect of the clay – but willing and receptive to God's impact on us. As we yield to God, He reshapes us into His valuable vessels. I prophesy, therefore, that every bit of your broken life shall be fixed by the LORD today. In Jesus' mighty name. Amen.

PRAYER POINTS:

1. Wonderful LORD, I thank You for being the Potter of my life.
2. I plead the blood of Jesus for cleansing and coverage, with faith for my victory. In the name of Jesus.
3. Holy Spirit, expose every evil contamination in my life and uproot it. In the name of Jesus.
4. Holy Ghost, uproot by Your fire every tare sown into the wheat of my life. In the name of Jesus.
5. LORD, destroy all legal ground for satanic invasion in my life. In the name of Jesus.
6. Holy Ghost fire, dry up the source of "potholes" or "erosion" in my life. In the name of Jesus.
7. LORD, paralyze the efforts of the Enemy to tamper with Your plan for my life. In the name of Jesus.

8. Dash all the wicked persecutors of my life into pieces like the potter's vessel, O LORD. In Jesus' name.

9. Potholes of sickness, poverty, failure, rejection, persecution, and unfruitfulness, I reject you! Vanish from my life and family. In the name of Jesus.

10. God, my Father, fix every pothole on the journey of my life. In the name of Jesus.

11. LORD, break me down and remold me into Your vessel of honour. In the name of Jesus.

12. LORD, be my roadmap and make me remain focused on my journey of life. In the name of Jesus.

13. My Father and my God increase my love, faith, and trust in You. In the name of Jesus.

14. The plan and purpose of the LORD for my life shall not be aborted. In the name of Jesus.

15. LORD, I thank You for answering my prayers and Your new design for my life. In the name of Jesus.

PRAYER 17

JESUS WILL MEND YOUR BROKEN LIFE

BIBLE VERSES: *Matthew 15:24-31; Acts 10:48*

INTRODUCTION

- - A broken life is that which is no longer normal for various reasons.
- - Genesis 1:31 speaks of perfection in the creation of God including human beings.
- - Some of the reasons for broken lives, which came up and developed after creation include
    a) satanic wickedness
    b) sin
    c) ignorance
    d) carelessness

Examples of broken lives include:
  a) Those in Matthew 15:24-31
  b) Demonic man in Mark 5:1-15

c) Woman with the issue of blood in Mark 5:25-34
d) Widow of Nain in Luke 7:13-16
e) Woman caught in adultery in John 8:1-11

- - The truth is Jesus Christ during His earthly ministry went about healing many people and mending several broken lives (Acts 10:38). On His departure, He gave believers the authority to do the same (John 14:12-14).
- - Believers are expected to bring those who need the same work (healing deliverance) in their lives to receive the touch of Jesus Christ through the testimony of Jesus and prayers. Jesus Christ will do the same in your life today as you pray to God in His name.
- - Before you begin to pray, however, you must believe all you have heard; sincerely surrender your life to Jesus Christ; promise to do away with sin; pursue righteousness, and trust Christ to heal and mend every broken aspect of your life. He will not fail you. In the mighty name of Jesus.

PRAYER POINTS:

1. LORD, I thank You for Your mighty power to save, heal, mend, and deliver broken lives.

2. I plead the blood of Jesus for cleansing and coverage. In the name of Jesus.
3. Anything standing on my foundation as an object of shame and reproach, be uprooted by the fire of God. In the name of Jesus.
4. LORD, create in me the living faith for my miracles today. In the name of Jesus.
5. Holy Ghost fire, consume every foundational curse operating in my life. In the name of Jesus.
6. Powers of my father's house assigned to derail my God-ordained destiny, in the name of Jesus.
7. Holy Spirit, uproot every form of ignorance and carelessness in my life. In the name of Jesus.
8. Blood of Jesus, nullify every satanic manipulation in my life. In the name of Jesus.
9. Great Physician, mend, heal, and restore my broken life. In the name of Jesus.
10. LORD, establish me in Your Word and power for spiritual strength. In the name of Jesus.
11. Send out Your light and let it lead me on my journey, O LORD. In the name of Jesus.
12. Let Your loving-kindness and truth continually preserve me, O LORD. In the name of Jesus.
13. God, my Father, build up my thoughts on things that edify rather than vain things. In the name of Jesus.

14. Make my life a testimony of Your miraculous touch, O LORD. In the name of Jesus.
15. LORD Jesus, I thank You for answering my prayers today. In the name of Jesus.

PRAYER 18

DESTROY THE WORK OF EVIL RE-CREATORS IN MY LIFE, O LORD

BIBLE VERSES: *Genesis 37:5-10, 18-20*

INTRODUCTION

God is the Creator of heaven and the earth including the people on the earth. He bestows on them extraordinary prosperity (Genesis 1:26-29). "And God saw everything that he had made, and, behold, it was very good" (Genesis 3:36). The evil re-creator is one who recreates things into another form, for example, turning what is good into bad.

God's Word also gave us an account of how the evil re-creator entered the world's scene and accomplished his work in the lives of the first human beings. In Genesis 3:1, the Devil appeared in the form of a serpent and deceived the first human beings. He stole their glory and recreated the destiny of the people into the most horrible state of suffering.

When we speak of evil re-creators, we can confidently refer to them as the Devil, his fallen angels (the demons), and human agents. Their main duty is to tamper with the good things God designed into the destiny of every human being. The evil re-creators are, in better words, destiny diverters.

The class or category of evil re-creators can be understood by analyzing the various aspects of their operations. However they appear, it will be to carry out the instructions of Satan:

a) Those who tamper with pregnancy (to abort, miscarry or meddle with the gender or other aspects of the pregnancy and the child in the womb).

b) The robbers of glory in children. When they are born, children are washed or carried by satanic agents who manipulate the head, eyes, ears or other vital organs of the child to dispossess the child of whatever glory is in his/her destiny. The story has been told of a wet sponge that was used to wash a man when he was a child. It was recovered from an old female member of the family after 38 years. This was possible by divine intervention in the life of the man who after completing his university education became wretched and jobless due to the manipulation of the evil re-creators.

c) Destiny oppressors can be enemies in the (i) household (ii) workplace (iii) society and (iv) spiritual houses including the church. Illustrations include:

    i.   Being barren through the theft of the victim's pants

    ii.   Failure in vital examinations after eating demonic food in the dream (spiritual houses where negative prophecies are released to divert one's destiny).

What to Do:

a) Do not be ignorant of evil re-creators. They were there from the beginning (2 Corinthians 2: 11).

b) Examine your spiritual standing. Surrender your life to Jesus Christ if not yet done (John 3:3)

c) Cast your burden upon the LORD (1 Peter 5:7)

d) In prayer to the LORD, ask Him to fight for you

2. Since the LORD is the unchanging changer, He alone has the capacity to destroy the works of the evil re-creators and restore His original destiny for your life and family. Call upon Him now.

PRAYER POINTS:

1. LORD, I thank You because of Your goodness and Your mercy that endures forever.

2. I plead the blood of Jesus and cover myself and my family with the blood. In the name of Jesus.
3. Holy Ghost, chase out every form of ignorance and unbelief in my life. In the name of Jesus.
4. Holy Ghost, remove every weakness or infirmity in my life and fill my prayers with Your fire. In the name of Jesus.
5. Holy Spirit, frustrate every satanic deception in my life. In the name of Jesus.
6. Grace for increased faith, fall upon me now. In the name of Jesus.
7. Evil strongman of my father's house assigned against my life, be paralyzed and die. In the name of Jesus.
8. Seed and properties of the evil re-creators in my life, be uprooted by the fire of God. In the name of Jesus.
9. Covenants of suffering and pain made by household enemies over my life and destiny, blood of Jesus break it. In the name of Jesus.
10. Let those that devise my hurt be turned back and brought to confusion. In the name of Jesus.
11. Evil river in my place of birth holding my destiny in bondage, release me and dry up from the source. In the name of Jesus.
12. LORD, expose and destroy every plan and deceit of the evil re-creators in my life and family. In the name of Jesus.

13. LORD, frustrate the desire, plan, and prayers of my enemy against my destiny. In the name of Jesus.
14. LORD, destroy the Adamic nature in my life and family. Change it to Your own. In the name of Jesus.
15. LORD, disgrace the evil re-creators in my life by Your uncommon miracles of prosperity today. In the name of Jesus.

PRAYER 19

EVIL DREAMS IN MY LIFE SHALL BE ABORTED

BIBLE VERSES: *Genesis 40:16-22*

INTRODUCTION

- Dreams are a series of pictures or events in a sleeping person's mind; something not real or not yet real. Dreams can be good, divine or evil and satanic.
- Dreams that come from God (divine) can be used to warn or reveal what is about to, or going to happen in the future (Genesis 28:12-17).
- Dreams from the Devil or dark kingdom are used as mediums to carry out evil works in human lives (John 10:10). For example, spending money in the dream is the way to make you poor.
- While we should claim good dreams and thank God for them, evil or satanic dreams should be rejected

and cancelled very quickly with the utmost intensity of the fire of the Holy Ghost and the Word of God.
- We are concerned here with evil or satanic dreams and how to cancel them. It is very important to consider the source of these dreams, which include (a) Satan (b) sin – mostly, thoughts that are not pure in the heart (c) foundational powers (d) household witchcraft, and enemies, to mention a few.
- As believers, we are expected to be aware of the Devil's plans and works (2 Corinthians 2:11) and be prepared at all times to cancel them even more in our dream life. Some of the weapons available for us to use include (a) the Word of God (b) the name and blood of Jesus (c) faith (d) holiness and righteousness (e) trust in God and (f) fervent prayers.
- Unbelievers must be genuinely born again first and then add all the above to cancel evil dreams. Unless evil or satanic dreams are promptly cancelled, they have the tendency to manipulate or manifest evil. The person will be left to blame him/herself for any calamity.
- For the evil dreams to be aborted, therefore, violent prayers are required to remove satanic control of our dreams (Matthew 11:12). I prophesy that the counsel of the enemies in your life shall not stand; your head shall not be hung on the altar of evil. You

shall be restored to good dreams and begin to possess your possessions. In Jesus' mighty name. Amen.

PRAYER POINTS:

1. God of all comfort, I bless and honour You for Your wonderful work in my life.
2. I plead the blood of Jesus Christ and cover myself with the blood. In the name of Jesus.
3. Blood of Jesus, flush out every evil contamination in my thoughts and dreams. In the name of Jesus.
4. Blood of Jesus, purge my system of demonic foods and drinks eaten in the dreams. In the name of Jesus.
5. Holy Ghost, uproot by Your fire every seed of sickness, affliction, and suffering planted into my life in the dreams. In the name of Jesus.
6. LORD, scatter the conspiracy of the wicked against my life by Your arrow. In the name of Jesus.
7. Every arrester in my dream, be arrested, chained and die by the fire of God. In the name of Jesus.
8. Dreams of demotion and anti-prosperity in my life, vanish forever! In the name of Jesus.
9. Holy Ghost fire, break the power of satanic dreams in my life. In the name of Jesus.
10. Holy Ghost fire, consume every spirit of death harassing me in the dream. In the name of Jesus.

11. LORD, fill my life and dreams with the anointing of fire. In the name of Jesus.
12. According to Isaiah 7:7, no evil dream shall stand or come to pass in my life. In the name of Jesus.
13. LORD, restore all the virtue, goodness, and blessings stolen by household witchcraft in my dreams. In the name of Jesus.
14. LORD, build Your wall of fire around me and my family. In the name of Jesus.
15. LORD, I thank You for answering these prayers by Your fire. In the name of Jesus.

PRAYER 20

WIPE OUT EVERY "BUT" IN MY LIFFE, O LORD

BIBLE VERSES: *2 Kings 5:1-8*

INTRODUCTION

- A "but" is anything in life that is shameful and disgraceful; humiliates; not normal, abnormal; reproachable; dehumanizing; bringing sorrow and anguish – physically or mentally; bringing dejection.
- Naaman's "but" was sickness or the disease of leprosy. Leprosy, much like AIDS of today, was one of the most feared diseases of the time because it was extremely contagious and incurable in many cases. It was terminal in the worst cases and required being quarantined in the lepers' camp.
- Some of life's problems are just like Naaman – disgraceful, reproachable or fearful.

- Medical science has tried to take care of some "buts" of life but how can doctors explain or cure emotional problems? How can they explain what happened when somebody loses a baby during pregnancy after seeing a red object in a dream? How can doctors determine why somebody has bad luck, fails in everything he or she handles or operates under a curse or covenants and so on?
- With his position as a great warrior, Naaman could afford the best physician in the world to cure him. Yet, he could not find a solution until he had a divine connection. He got in touch with the God of Elisha of Israel. It is instructive that at that time, Syria, the country to which Naaman belonged, and Israel were not good friends, but God was and still is the God of the entire human race.
- Until Naaman obeyed the word of God through the prophet Elisha, his problem remained. In the same way, some "buts" in peoples' lives require obedience to God's instructions.
- We may not always understand God's way of working but by humbly obeying Him, we will receive His blessings or deliverance. Note, however, that:
  1) God's ways are the best

2) God wants our obedience more than sacrifice or anything else

3) God responds to faith that comes from obedience to bless

4) God can use anything or anybody to accomplish his purpose

5) God requires total surrender from all those who come to Him for anything

- Therefore, as we reach out to God now and pour out our hearts to Him like Jabez in 1 Chronicles 4:10, He will arise in His mercy and wipe out all your "buts" to bring glory to His name. In Jesus' mighty name.

PRAYER POINTS:

1. Rock of Ages, I thank You for Your power to set me free from any bondage or captivity.
2. I plead the blood of Jesus to cleanse and uproot every spirit of pride in me. In the name of Jesus.
3. Holy Spirit, repair whatever damage ignorance and carelessness have done to my spiritual life. In the name of Jesus.
4. Whatever is the origin of stubborn problems in my life, LORD, dry them up. In the name of Jesus.

5. Rock of Ages, frustrate the arrow of evil words fired into my life and destiny by household enemies. In the name of Jesus.

6. LORD, disgrace and destroy all the wicked agents of the dark kingdom supervising affliction in my life. In the name of Jesus.

7. I command the evil loads designed to weigh down my spiritual strength to be carried by their maker. In the name of Jesus.

8. LORD, destroy by Your fire every instrument of reproach and persecution in my life. In the name of Jesus.

9. Every "but" that came into my life through satanic manipulation, be wiped out by the blood of Jesus. In Jesus' name.

10. Holy Ghost, separate me from and uproot every "but" in my life that has its origin in my foundation. In the name of Jesus.

11. Spirits of obedience and faith, come upon me and position me for my miracles. In the name of Jesus.

12. Blood of Jesus, cancel evil decisions made in the coven of witchcraft and familiar spirits concerning my life. In the name of Jesus.

13. LORD, command Your warring angels to restore to me now every good thing the Enemy has taken away from me by deceit. In the name of Jesus.

14. LORD, build Your wall of fire around all those beautiful things You have done in my life. In the name of Jesus.
15. Covenant-keeping God, renew Your covenant of good health, help, favour, progress, and peace in my life and family. In the name of Jesus.

PRAYER 21

RECEIVING POWER FOR WEALTH AND PROSPERITY

BIBLE VERSES: *Deuteronomy 8:17-18; Joshua 1:7-9; Psalm 112:1-3*

INTRODUCTION

- Power is the ability to do something. Wealth is the abundance of possessions including money, while prosperity is to flourish (do well) financially. Therefore, to receive the power for wealth and prosperity is the ability to have abundant possessions or money and flourish financially.
- God, in creating heaven and the earth endowed human beings with unlimited resources on the earth (Genesis 1:26-29). Thus, He became the source of all things including wealth and prosperity.
- The desire, inclination, and quest of the people of the world for wealth and prosperity have become so strong, they are desperate and will go anywhere or

to any length to do anything – fair or unfair – in search of wealth and prosperity. Despite concerted efforts of human beings in this regard, success has remained an unrealistic hope. This is not surprising because, to a large extent, human poverty and the insatiable quest for wealth and prosperity originated through the curse received for disobedience in Genesis 3:14-19.

- The truth is at the point of the expulsion of human beings from the privilege of abundance, even until now, God retained the absolute control of all things. The Devil deceived and continues to employ all the strategies of deception to ensure God does not win any of His projects for human beings. He does so by making them not believe the promises of God. In the world today, many believe in money, but money can fail. Because of the unreliable nature of money (Proverbs 13:11), they turn to acquiring properties and possessions, many times to their peril. God remains the source and giver of all good, enduring wealth, and prosperity (Deuteronomy 8:18).

- Despite all the failures in the world, God remains strong, powerful, and at hand to fulfil all the desires and expectations of His people. Waiting upon God to receive power and prosperity becomes possible and easy for believers because of their faith in God (Psalm 112:1-3). Faith in God must include faith in His timing, patience, and endurance.

- As you obey His directive to become one of His children – if you are not one yet – rise up in prayers now and receive the power for wealth and prosperity from Him. In Jesus' mighty name. Amen.

PRAYER POINTS:

1. The all-sufficient God, I bless You for Your capacity to empower me for wealth and prosperity.
2. Dip me in Your blood for total cleansing and coverage, O LORD. In the name of Jesus.
3. LORD, break and cancel every ancestral curse troubling my faith in You. In the name of Jesus.
4. LORD, create in me the faith and strength to be patient to receive Your power for wealth and prosperity. In the name of Jesus.
5. Holy Ghost fire, burn to ashes all the properties of familiar spirits and witchcraft in my possession, which serve as doors for monitoring and manipulation. In the name of Jesus.
6. Blood of Jesus, break and nullify every occultic spell or agreement made with the dark kingdom against my prosperity. In the name of Jesus.

7. Holy Spirit, silence forever every evil voice speaking against my wealth and prosperity. In the name of Jesus.

8. LORD, send Your angel Michael to release any power that has arrested the angels of my blessings. In the name of Jesus.

9. Holy Ghost, break down every satanic cage, bank or stronghold holding my finances and set them free. In the name of Jesus.

10. Any of my goodness, wealth, and prosperity in the hands of oppressors or tormentors, Holy Ghost, torment them to return all to me. In the name of Jesus.

11. LORD, give me the keys to good success in my handiwork. In the name of Jesus.

12. LORD, put all the enemies of my breakthrough to permanent shame. In the name of Jesus.

13. As I build, I shall inhabit. As I plant, I shall eat to the full. In the name of Jesus.

14. Henceforth, my family and I shall no more labour in vain. In the name of Jesus.

15. LORD, I thank You for Your answer to my prayers and the receipt of the power for wealth and prosperity. In the name of Jesus.

PRAYER 22

DELIVER ME FROM THE MENTALITY OF "NOT ENOUGH" AND "NOT AT ALL," O LORD

BIBLE VERSES: *Hebrews 13:5-6; Matthew 14:15-21*

INTRODUCTION

- "Not enough" and "not at all" are negative words of confession capable of putting anyone who speaks them into permanent poverty.
- The original plan of God for human beings was and still is to live in abundance (Genesis 1:26–29).
- The Devil, through deceit, seduced the first people created to disobey God. In doing this, the realm of abundance was lost, and they fell into the realm of poverty, sickness, and ultimate death. But through the love of God and His work in sending Jesus Christ into the world to redeem the world, the

human race regained its original glory and abundance.

- The reality of the matter, however, is that despite the redemption by Jesus Christ and His poverty (2 Corinthians 8:9), some believers (Christians) still operate under the mentality of "not enough" or "not at all." Why? Because this category of people believe their condition of living is due to:
  a) The nature of their birth, that is, born into poor families
  b) Punishment for their sins
  c) The actions of the Enemy

The battle rages on.

- While to some extent the above may be true, they are in no way the whole truth.
- The Word of God teaches us as believers (those born again and delivered from the power of Satan and sin), that,
- (a) We must not worry about any of our needs (Matthew 6:25, 31). To worry is to allow a thing to gain control of the mind negatively
- (b) We must be content with what we have (Hebrews 13:5). We become content when we are aware of God's sufficiency to meet our needs.

Believers who become materialistic are saying God cannot take care of them or, at least, that He won't take care of them in the way they want

- (c) We must be faithful in our giving to God and others (Malachi 3:10; Luke 6:38). Whatever we give to the LORD whether it is talent, time, money or treasure, He will use and multiply. When we give to the LORD, we can experience multiplication in our resources.
- (d) We must allow the LORD to lead us into our harvest of supplies (Psalm 32:8). When we do this, He will not only lead us but also give the power to get wealth and protect us in our abundance.
- (e) We must prayerfully reach out to God for our needs (Philippians 4:6). As we do this, we must trust God for action. As He makes our needs available, we must thank Him for all we receive from Him.
- When we believe the above truth of God's Word and pray along the line, then we can subdue and overcome the mentality of "not enough" and "not at all."
- Before you pray, it is very important to reflect on your relationship with Jesus Christ. If it is not right, seize this opportunity to speak to Him. Ask Him to forgive and wash your sins away with His blood. Be

assured that your deliverance is settled. In Jesus' mighty name.

PRAYER POINTS:

1. Ever faithful God, I magnify Your holy name for Your power to bless me abundantly.
2. I plead the blood of Jesus Christ for total cleansing and coverage. In the name of Jesus.
3. Ancestral chain of poverty and wretchedness in my life, break by the fire of God. In the name of Jesus.
4. Any power limiting my ability to receive from the abundance of God, die by fire. In the name of Jesus.
5. Environmental factors causing me despair and worry about virtually everything, be chased out of my life and family. In the name of Jesus.
6. Holy Ghost, uproot the fear of the unknown programmed into my mind by the Devil. In the name of Jesus.
7. Whatever damage unbelief has done in my life, LORD, repair it. In the name of Jesus.
8. Conspiracy of the dark kingdom against my faith, hope, and trust in the promises of God for my life, be scattered by the fire of God. In the name of Jesus.

9. Blood of Jesus, flush out the evil thought of "not enough" and "not at all" from my heart. In Jesus' name.

10. Anywhere my life and goodness are being held hostage, LORD, command Your warring angels to locate and liberate them. In the name of Jesus.

11. LORD, fill my heart with the truth of Your Word continually. In the name of Jesus.

12. However small that lack, pain, and suffering may be, I shall no more taste them. In the name of Jesus.

13. LORD, renew the covenant of abundance and wealth in my life. In the name of Jesus.

14. The season of fruitfulness and abundance shall not cease in my life. In the name of Jesus.

15. LORD, I thank You for the answer to my prayers and the flow of divine provisions. In the name of Jesus.

PRAYER 23

MEET MY NEEDS, O LORD!

BIBLE VERSES: *Psalm 23:1-6; Philippians 4:19*

INTRODUCTION

- God is the creator of all things, times, and seasons including human beings and their needs. Because of the times and seasons, there are also peculiar needs. Human beings have the tendency to be troubled by their needs. It is one of the products of the curse incurred by Adam and Eve, the first people created by God in the garden of Eden (Genesis 3:17-19). Thus, from that point in time up to the present, the thought of meeting their needs has made people anxious to put things together to meet these needs.
- The institution of governments in various nations of the world is designed to meet, to an extent, the needs of the people. This is supposed to be done by providing infrastructures required for the people to produce financial resources to acquire their needs.

However, to a large extent, governments have failed in this respect. Even in most African societies, governments have turned out to be major hindrances to God-given resources flowing properly into the lives of the people. For example, high levels of corruption have prevented many mineral resources from providing social benefits to the people.

- The effect of the above is that the people are placed in a state of worry and agitation for virtually every need of life. As human beings, our needs include the following:

a) Salvation

b) Provision

c) Protection

d) Healing

e) Fruitfulness

f) Prosperity

g) Deliverance

h) Success

i) Victory

j) Peace

Five of these needs will be highlighted here:

(a) Salvation (John 3:3, 5) is the key or gate to enter the kingdom of God; failure to enter will keep a person in the category of dogs.

(b) Provision (Philippians 4:19) is our day-to-day food. The absence of this is a sign of poverty. Poverty is the Devil's instrument to prove to people God is not real.

(c) Healing (Psalm 107:20) is what is needed when a person is not physically sound. Sickness is the Devil's handiwork to torment and kill people prematurely.

(d) Fruitfulness (Deuteronomy 7:14) is the bearing of fruits in every area of human endeavour including childbearing. Unfruitfulness is the Devil's work to frustrate and keep people in perpetual agony at home and work.

(e) Peace (John 14:27) is the absence of crises. A crisis is a sign that life, home, work, church, nation, etc. is not at peace.

- Worrying about our needs is pointless because doing so cannot fill them. God knows our needs and promises to meet the ones that are real – not necessarily all our desires. Jesus Christ wants us to have faith in God for all our needs by miracles or otherwise (Mark 11:22). However small your faith is, God will put fire into it. As you call upon Him now, the miracle of divine supply will start to happen in your life now.

- Before we pray and ask for anything, the LORD Jesus Christ asked us to seek first the kingdom of God and His righteousness. Therefore, make this a very important aspect of your life and get ready for the rain of God's blessings now. There shall be no further delay. In Jesus' mighty name. Amen.

PRAYER POINTS:

1. All-sufficient God, I thank You for revealing Yourself as the only and unfailing source of my needs.
2. I plead the blood of Jesus for total cleansing and coverage. In the name of Jesus.
3. Any aspect of my life, which I have kept away from You, LORD, by Your mercy, take it over now. In the name of Jesus.
4. Whatever the enemies have done to my life to block the flow of God's blessings, LORD, neutralize them. In the name of Jesus.
5. Any gathering of household witchcraft to decide and decree problems into my life, LORD, scatter them and reverse their decree. In the name of Jesus.

6. Holy Ghost Fire, dismantle every stronghold, hindrance or delay set up against my fruitfulness. In the name of Jesus.

7. Blood of Jesus, flush out every disease-carrying parasite and sickness in my body. In the name of Jesus.

8. Holy Ghost, arrest every spiritual and physical robber in my life; recover and return all that has been stolen. In the name of Jesus.

9. Blood of Jesus, break and cancel all the curses of poverty and unfruitfulness by any occult consultant in my life. In the name of Jesus.

10. Every satanic attack on my faith and trust in You, LORD, destroy them. In the name of Jesus.

11. LORD, visit me now and show Yourself mighty in my situation. In the name of Jesus.

12. My LORD and my God, open Your hands now and satisfy all my desires. In the name of Jesus.

13. I shall never lack any good thing as the righteousness of God in Christ Jesus. In the name of Jesus.

14. I confess that the LORD, as the source of my needs, shall never be tired of me. In the name of Jesus.

15. LORD, I thank You for answering my prayers and the testimony that will follow. In the name of Jesus.

PRAYER 24

RECOVERING ALL THE ENEMIES HAVE STOLEN

BIBLE VERSES: *1 Samuel 30:1-9, 18-20*

INTRODUCTION

- The Bible says: "Be sober, be vigilant, because your adversary the devil, as a roaring lion, walketh about, seeking whom he may devour" (1 Peter 5:8). Judging by his action in Genesis Chapter 1, the Devil took the form of the serpent to deceive Adam and Eve, the first human beings on earth. He robbed them of the pleasure and glory they enjoyed in the garden of Eden (Romans 3:23).
- In John 10:10, Jesus Christ described the Devil as a thief. The Devil is the head of the fallen angels sent out of heaven because of disobedience. He and these angels continue to operate in the spiritual realm. Through his human agents, he still carries on his work on the earth among human beings.

- You can know if a person is working for the Devil and his dark kingdom if the works in the person resemble those of the Devil in all forms of wickedness including robbery and destruction. When the spirit of the Devil enters anyone, the only thing that is commonly noticed is the desire to kill, steal, and destroy.
- Just like the Amalekites in the Bible verses, those who belong to the Devil will always carry out their activities to put people in problems of various dimensions. Unsuspecting believers will always fall into the snares of the Devil and his agents. How can the following be explained?

    (a) The occult man who cast spells upon the neighbour's child to kill him or her. The mother of the child discovers the secret and delivers her child through serious prayer.

    (b) Robbing another person's life-saving property through satanic manipulation

    (c) Robbing another person's exalted position through satanic deception

    (d) A lecturer cutting the marks of a lady in her final examination because of her failure to agree to an immoral relationship

(e) Conspiracy of elders in the church to refuse to pay the pastor's salary. Thus, preventing the pastor from paying his children's school fees and almost costing him his life when he could not buy drugs during sickness. The list can be endless.

Every believer should know what to do to protect him/herself from the activities of the Devil and his agents where, by deceit, they have entered to steal and recover what they stole. The example of David in our Bible verse is a good one. Therefore, as you go to God in prayer put your request to Him. Set your mind on His ability to resolve the matter in your favour. He will also restore to you all the enemies have stolen. You will continue to possess your possessions (Obadiah 17). In Jesus' mighty name. Amen.

PRAYER POINTS:

1. My Father and God, I magnify Your holy name because You are a very present help in trouble.
2. I soak myself in the blood of Jesus for total cleansing and coverage. In the name of Jesus.
3. Anything I did wrong that opened the door for the Enemy to operate, LORD, by Your mercy, cancel it by the blood of Jesus. In Jesus' name.

4. Holy Spirit, expose the deceit and manipulation of the Devil and his agents in my life and disgrace them. In the name of Jesus.

5. Every instrument of discouragement planted by the Devil's agents into my life, be destroyed by the fire of God. In the name of Jesus.

6. LORD, expose and disgrace every unfriendly friend in my life and family. In the name of Jesus.

7. Holy Ghost thunder, break open the satanic warehouse holding my goodness and blessings and restore them to me. In the name of Jesus.

8. I pursue, overtake, and recover all my property, health, joy, prosperity, glory, and peace stolen by the enemies. In the name of Jesus.

9. LORD, build the wall of Your fire around me and my family. In the name of Jesus.

10. LORD, clothe me with Your garment of strong faith, holiness, and righteousness. In the name of Jesus.

11. My mouth shall never co-operate with my enemies to steal my peace. In the name of Jesus.

12. The Word of God shall fortify me and be effective in the solution of my problems. In the name of Jesus.

13. LORD, silence the oppressors in my life forever. In the name of Jesus.

14. My health and strength shall not fail in the task of taking my rightful place in God's kingdom. In the name of Jesus.
15. LORD, I thank You for answering my prayers and rising up early to help me. In the name of Jesus.

PRAYER 25

BREAK THE TEETH OF THE UNGODLY IN MY LIFE, O LORD

BIBLE VERSES: *Psalm 3:6-8; 58:1-7*

INTRODUCTION

The ungodly are wicked people who strive with you, think evil of you, wish evil on you, and do evil to you. They also join others to rejoice in your trouble, fight against your finances, health, progress, success, joy, and peace.

Believers in Christ should not find it difficult to identify the ungodly. However, due to insensitivity, lack of discernment, and most often, laziness in the study of God's Word and prayers, the identity of the ungodly or wicked is hidden from them for a long time.

These ungodly or wicked people are commonly known in their various operations or capacities as witches and wizards, strongmen or strongwomen, familiar spirits, occult personalities, household enemies, and unfriendly friends.

Their identities, therefore, are revealed in their various activities.

The truth is that these people who are agents of the dark kingdom play a lot of destructive roles in the affairs of mankind. They do not mind their own affairs but are negatively interested in the affairs of other people. It is very sad that people, despite the awareness provided by the Word of God, still allow their lives and affairs to be manipulated by these evil people.

When you deal with them as God wants them to be dealt with, you will live a peaceful and victorious life as a child of God. They will use their teeth to bite you and your destiny. However, as you report them to the LORD in prayer now, He will arise, break their teeth, and deliver you completely. In the name of Jesus. Before you pray, look into your life and if it is not right with God, repent of any shortcoming. Ask God for mercy then surrender your life totally to the LORD Jesus Christ and receive power from His blood.

PRAYER POINTS:

1. Mighty Warrior, I worship you for what You are and what you will do in my life today.
2. I plead the precious blood of Jesus for total cleansing and coverage. In the name of Jesus.
3. Holy Spirit, fill and endue me with Your power for my victory today. In the name of Jesus.

4. Rock of Ages, break to pieces every stronghold of witchcraft in my life and family. In the name of Jesus.

5. Holy Ghost, expose and destroy every dark work done against me in the secret. In the name of Jesus.

6. My Father and defender, break the teeth of the ungodly in my life and family. In the name of Jesus.

7. Arrest and break the bands of the wicked that are arresting my progress, O LORD. In the name of Jesus.

8. LORD, dry up every source of pain and sorrow in my life and family. In the name of Jesus.

9. LORD, cancel every curse or counsel of untimely death in my life and family. In the name of Jesus.

10. By the authority of heaven, I command the pit dug by my enemies for me to become their grave. In the name of Jesus.

11. LORD, overturn every device of my adversaries and disgrace them. In the name of Jesus.

12. Render all wicked oppressors and destroyers in my life powerless and chase them out, in the name of Jesus.

13. Keep me as the apple of the eye and hide me under Your shadow, O LORD. In the name of Jesus.

14. Clothe me with Your power and make my life a terror to the dark kingdom. In the name of Jesus.

15. LORD, be glorified for Your great power of deliverance in my life today. In the name of Jesus.

PRAYER 26

BREAK THE CURSE OF FAILURE AND POVERTY, O LORD

BIBLE VERSES: Numbers 22:1-6; 1 Chronicles 4:9-10

INTRODUCTION

- The dictionary defines "curse" as a solemn utterance intended to invoke the supernatural power to inflict harm or punishment on someone or something. Also, "failure" is the absence of success, while "poverty" is the state of being extremely poor. In other words, a curse is the opposite of a blessing. Failure is the opposite of success, while poverty is the opposite of wealth.
- In the spiritual realm for which we are concerned here, a curse is any statement, pronouncement or call for evil to come upon a person or thing with or without a reason. A curse can be invoked face-to-face or in the spirit with no one noticing it. A curse can be "deserved" or "undeserved." It is done to a

person "with cause" or "without cause." A curse can be invoked on anyone by another person, diviner, sorcerer or God. It is very important to note here that the consequences of a curse are failure and poverty.

- In Numbers Chapter 22, Balak, because of fear, requested Balaam to curse the Israelites without them knowing, but they escaped the curse by divine intervention. In 1 Chronicles 4:9, the words of Jabez's mother became a curse to him. It is not very clear whether the mother of Jabez was aware of the effect her statement would have on her son. Jabez later realized the implications of his mother's statement in his situation. He prayed and received divine deliverance.

- A curse can enter anyone's life and, particularly, for the purpose of this prayer, we will look at the entrances of (a) sin (b) bearing evil names (c) evil locations or activities or (d) undeserved. As can be seen, our two examples fall under the category of "undeserved." The beauty of the matter is that the two curses were divinely frustrated. Therefore, any curse of failure and poverty standing against your life shall be broken. In Jesus' name.

- It is important to note here that when the effects of a curse begin to show up in anyone's life, there is a serious need to call upon God as Jabez did. As you pray with strong faith and your stand in Jesus Christ made right, I prophesy that every curse of failure and poverty in your life shall be broken and cancelled. In Jesus' mighty name. Amen.

PRAYER POINTS:

1. Unchangeable changer, I magnify Your name for Your power to perfect all about me.
2. LORD, any sin of disobedience in my life, forgive and cancel it by Your blood. In the name of Jesus.
3. I plead the blood of Jesus to cleanse and stand for my defense today. In the name of Jesus.
4. Whatever I have done to deserve a curse, LORD, by Your mercy and blood cancel it. In Jesus' name.
5. LORD, disgrace any strongman using satanic authority over my life. In the name of Jesus.
6. Any curse, prophecy or statement issued into my life and destiny, backfire! In the name of Jesus.
7. Powers of darkness cursing my destiny day and night, you are liars. Die by fire. In the name of Jesus.
8. Curse of failure and poverty in my handiwork, break by the blood of Jesus. In the name of Jesus.
9. Blood of Jesus, restore any good thing that I have lost due to a curse. In the name of Jesus.

10. Fire of poverty set up by household enemies for my life, consume your maker. In the name of Jesus.

11. LORD, silence the mocking and reproach of my enemies by Your favour on me. In the name of Jesus.

12. Curse of untimely death operating in my foundation, be broken by the blood of Jesus. In Jesus' name.

13. LORD, frustrate the token of liars in my family and turn their wisdom into foolishness. In Jesus' name.

14. The LORD shall position me for all-round prosperity in my handiwork. In the name of Jesus.

15. LORD, I thank You for answers to my prayers and the testimonies to follow. In the name of Jesus.

PRAYER 27

WALKING OUT OF THE FIRE OF AFFLICTION

BIBLE VERSES: Isaiah 43:1-3; Daniel 3:16-25

INTRODUCTION

The fire of affliction represents problems, difficulties or anything in life that runs contrary to peace and prosperity such as chronic sickness, extreme poverty, persistent failure, persecution, reproach, late marriage, barrenness, and loss of vital things through satanic wickedness.

God created Israel and made her special to Him. He also promised to protect them in times of trouble. Believers in Christ are also special and important to God as children. They can enter and go through the fire of affliction caused by satanic manipulation. Satan's intention is to weaken and cause them to grow cold or destroy them by drowning.

The LORD has promised He will be there when any believer passes through fire (Isaiah 43:2). However, anyone who goes through the fire of affliction in his/her own strength without the LORD is bound to be consumed.

Daniel 3:16-17 records the glaring case of the three Hebrews Shadrach, Meshach, and Abednego. Standing on their faith and confidence in God, they:

a) Defied the heathen king
b) Refused to bow to the idol set up by the king
c) Preferred to die instead
d) Were thrown into the burning fiery fire

They did not die but came out of the fire unhurt. In the end, they were promoted. Verse 25 also records the king's observation of the fourth person in the fire – the Son of God. This clearly confirms the promise of the presence of God when believers pass through any form of fire.

Whatever the name or kind of fire you are passing through; whatever the degree or temperature of the problem or affliction (Daniel 3:19), the LORD is telling you He is with you. You are walking out of it in grand style now. In Jesus' name.

Are you a child of God? If not, believe in Him now and stand on the promises of God as you pray for your deliverance.

PRAYER POINTS:

1. LORD, I thank You for Your presence in my life and the victory that awaits me today.
2. Divine God, put out the fire of affliction kindled by the Enemy for me and my family. In the name of Jesus.
3. LORD, be with me and lead me out of any fire of affliction or trial of faith. In the name of Jesus.
4. Holy Ghost fire, uproot whatever the wicked ones have planted into my life that sparked a fire in my life. In the name of Jesus.
5. Every battle, suffering, and problem flowing from the foundation of my life, LORD, quench it by Your own fire. In the name of Jesus.
6. LORD, let those who wish me evil be driven backward and put to shame. In the name of Jesus.
7. LORD, let those who seek my soul to destroy it be confounded and disgraced. In the name of Jesus.
8. Blood of Jesus, frustrate every plan of the Enemy to weaken me spiritually or put me out of circulation through dream attacks. In the name of Jesus.
9. LORD, scatter by Your fire every gathering of the Enemy and his evil consultants over my life and family. In the name of Jesus.

10. LORD, wipe out by Your blood any evil name given to me by the enemies. In the name of Jesus.

11. LORD, deliver me not unto the will and devices of my enemies. In the name of Jesus.

12. LORD, close every door of sorrow and pain in my life. In the name of Jesus.

13. With Your presence in my life and situation, LORD, make me walk out of all trouble gracefully. In the name of Jesus.

14. Wind and fire of God, blow out every fire of affliction in my life and family. In the name of Jesus.

15. LORD, I thank You for answering my prayer by Your fire. In the name of Jesus.

PRAYER 28

EVIL PATTERNS IN MY LIFE MUST EXPIRE

BIBLE VERSES: Lamentations 5:7-9

INTRODUCTION

Evil brings sorrow, distress or misfortune. A pattern is a regular occurrence or sequences of events. Evil patterns, therefore, are regular occurrences or sequence of events that bring sorrow, distress or misfortune.

Examples of evil patterns include bondage or captivity, slavery or servitude, retrogression and set back, stagnation, limitation, frustration, late marriage, barrenness, sickness, infirmity, affliction, and premature death.

- - The origins of evil patterns include the sin of disobedience, satanic wickedness, idolatry, occultism, witchcraft, curses, and covenants (flowing from evil words and statements or agreement entered by anyone or family), inherited problems (sickness, poverty, punishment for an offense of one member of the family, which automatically fall upon subsisting family members), and environmental troubles (prevalent problems operating in the locality).

- - The people of Israel and Judah represent major examples of evil patterns. Through the sin of disobedience and idolatry, they went into captivity – first Israel and later Judah. The two of them belong to the same family of the nation of Israel. Thus, when the life of any one or those of the family or group of people reflects any of the above examples, they are said to be going through evil patterns.

- - Evil patterns in the life of anyone or group of people cannot produce good results, only disastrous consequences. Hence, it is something that must be seriously dealt with when it is discovered.

- - Like the people of Israel and Judah, anyone seeking deliverance from evil patterns must genuinely repent of his/her sin or the sins of the family or group of people. Then the person must pray by faith for divine intervention. The merciful and powerful God is more than able to deliver to the uttermost.

PRAYER POINTS:

1. Merciful God, I honour Your most holy name for Your awesome power to deliver.
2. I repent of every sin of disobedience, idolatry, and unbelief in my life. I plead for mercy and the cleansing of the blood of Jesus. In Jesus' name.
3. Evil curse or covenant of my ancestors contending with God's destiny for my life, break. In the name of Jesus.
4. Blood of Jesus, destroy every evil possession from the womb that puts me under the evil pattern of servitude. In the name of Jesus.
5. LORD, cancel the evil name given by the Enemy that does not belong to me. In the name of Jesus.
6. Evil deposits into my life through demonic foods or drinks taken in the dream to mess up my life, blood of Jesus, flush them out. In the name of Jesus.
7. Holy Ghost, wipe out stagnation, limitation, and poverty that flowed from the evil pattern operating in my environment by Your fire. In the name of Jesus.
8. Blood of Jesus, wipe out every form of barrenness or unfruitfulness from my foundation. In the name of Jesus.

9. Sickness, infirmity, and affliction flowing from the evil pattern of my father's house, dry up now! In Jesus' name.

10. Evil pattern of premature and untimely death operating in my environment, my life is not your candidate. Be wiped out by the blood of Jesus. In Jesus' name.

11. LORD, frustrate every plan or design of the Enemy to change my destiny into evil patterns. In the name of Jesus.

12. God, arise and change for the best whatever is wrong in my life and destiny. In the name of Jesus.

13. LORD, clothe me with the garment of favour and dumbfounding breakthrough. In the name of Jesus.

14. I ask these prayers in faith and thank You LORD for Your prompt answer. In the name of Jesus.

PRAYER 29

EVIL TRANSACTIONS OVER MY LIFE SHALL FAIL

BIBLE VERSES: Genesis 37:23-28

INTRODUCTION

The world in which we live is full of jealousy and hatred. It is not a surprise to all that are close to the Bible.

In our Bible verses, pure jealousy made the brothers of Joseph decide to kill him. They were envious of the special love his father had for him, the dress from their father, and Joseph's dreams. Joseph became the object of the transaction with the Midianites. He was eventually sold to them and then to Potiphar in Egypt. Joseph's father, Jacob, was deceived into believing Joseph had been killed by evil beasts (Genesis 37:32, 33). However, because the LORD had the plan and purpose for Joseph's higher honour, He allowed the transaction and sale to succeed.

As a result of someone's hatred and jealousy, Joseph eventually found himself in prison in Egypt for an offense he did not commit. Even though the transaction done by Joseph's brothers seemed successful to them, and Joseph passed through very difficult times, God was in absolute control. In the end, Joseph became the second in command to Pharaoh in Egypt. His brothers' evil intentions failed. They could not frustrate his dreams.

Joseph's brothers went to Egypt in search of food in the famine and miraculously found Joseph in control of the food affairs in Egypt. Although Joseph had the power to repay his brothers for their past evil, he forgave and helped them. Joseph and his father were eventually reunited with infinite joy.

Recent happenings all over the world: terrorism, satanic and household wickedness, kidnapping, and demand for ransom are a few ways one's life can fall into evil transactions. Many evil arrangements are made in the spirit realm by witchcraft and household enemies. I pray, however, that every evil transaction over your life and family shall fail. It shall lead to your promotion, honour, and glory. In Jesus' wonderful name.

Note well that Joseph was able to overcome all the plans and desires of his enemies through his unwavering faith in God. Therefore, be encouraged by the ability of Joseph's God to deliver him and build your faith in the omnipotent, omniscient, and omnipresent God to frustrate every evil transaction in your life when you pray. Before you pray, however, make sure your life is surrendered to Jesus Christ promising to live and trust Him to the end. Your miracle is on the way and shall surely manifest in Jesus' mighty name. Amen.

PRAYER POINTS:

1. Ever faithful LORD, I bless and honour You because I know you are always with me.
2. I plead the blood of Jesus for total cleansing and coverage. In the name f Jesus.
3. Holy Spirit, fill me with unwavering faith like Joseph and Job. In the name of Jesus.
4. Every covenant or vow of my forefathers contrary to my divine destiny, loose your hold on my life. In the name of Jesus.
5. Holy Ghost fire, break every power of the household enemies of my father's house. In the name of Jesus.
6. LORD, frustrate every plan of my enemies to trade with my life and glory. In the name of Jesus.
7. LORD, deliver me from the deceitful and unjust people of my father's house. In the name of Jesus.
8. Anything that makes my heart bitter or sorrowful, LORD, uproot it by fire. In the name of Jesus.

9. Whatever aspect of my life is damaged by satanic wickedness, LORD, repair it now. In the name of Jesus.

10. As You did in the life of Joseph, turn every evil plan of my enemies into promotion and glory for me. In the name of Jesus.

11. Powers that want me to serve my enemies, you are liars. Be consumed by the fire of God. In the name of Jesus.

12. God, arise and contend with all those calling my name for evil in their prayers. In the name of Jesus.

13. LORD, bring the evil strongman in my life and family into open shame. In the name of Jesus.

14. Begin Your mighty work in my life to change my story to Your glory, O LORD. In the name of Jesus.

15. God of glory, I thank You for Your miracles manifested in my life today. In the name of Jesus.

PRAYER 30

WILDERNESS WANDERINGS IN MY LIFE SHALL EXPIRE

BIBLE VERSES: *Psalm 81:8-16*

INTRODUCTION

Wilderness wandering is a time or condition of hardship, suffering, pain, inconvenience, uncertainties, unhappiness, discomfort, etc., to mention just a few. Wilderness wandering, therefore, is not a pleasant time or desirable experience.

As we clearly see from the above, no one, not even believers (those who are children of God) desire wilderness wanderings. The truth, however, is that many people are going through what can be described as wilderness wandering at the present time. Poverty (serious lack), long periods of unemployment, chronic and life-threatening sicknesses, unfruitfulness, persecution, reproach, rejection, loss of good fortunes or loved ones can lead people into serious wanderings in the wilderness of life.

Despite the covenant of God with Abraham, his descendants had to experience wilderness wanderings (Numbers 14:33). In 2 Samuel 9:4, Mephibosheth, the surviving son of Jonathan, Saul's son was abandoned as a cripple man to wander about in Lo-debar (interpreted to mean barren).

Due to disobedience, God let Israel wander for forty years in the wilderness, instead of completing a journey meant to be eleven days (incredible).

Sometimes God allows people to continue in their stubbornness to bring them to their senses. He does not keep people from rebelling because He wants them to learn the consequences of sin. He uses these unpleasant experiences to turn people away from greater sin into faith in Him. Apostle James asks us to turn our hardships and pains into times of learning and praying. Tough times can teach us patience and faith in God (James 1:3-4).

God had promised in His covenant to restore His people if they would listen and return to Him (Exodus 23:22-27; Leviticus 26:3-13; Deuteronomy 7:12-26). We can look at the Bible verses to confirm some of His promises. Therefore, as you pray and ask God to help you solve your problems, promising to obey and trust Him, He will arise for your sake and cause all your wilderness wanderings to expire now. In Jesus' mighty name. Also, allow Him, Jesus Christ to take total control and direction of your life right now.

PRAYER POINTS:

1. Covenant-keeping God, I worship and honour You for Your power to save and deliver.
2. I plead the blood of Jesus Christ and cover my family and myself with the blood. In the name of Jesus.
3. In the abundance of Your mercy, O LORD, forgive all disobedience and murmurings in my life. In the name of Jesus.
4. Any ancestral curse leading me into wilderness wanderings, blood of Jesus break it. In the name of Jesus.
5. Any evil occurrence that turns my environment and place of living into a wilderness, blood of Jesus, wipe it out. In the name of Jesus.
6. Anything or power pushing me into error to always annoy God, Holy Ghost fire destroy it. In the name of Jesus.
7. Every evil voice assigned to silence me, O LORD God of Elijah, arise and silence it. In the name of Jesus.
8. LORD, tear off every veil of darkness from my eyes that makes me wander in the wilderness. In the name of Jesus.
9. Let all those who seek after my life to destroy it be confounded and put to shame, O LORD. In the name of Jesus.

10. Any infirmity that came into my life in the dream making me to wander about for a solution, LORD, uproot from my life by the blood of Jesus. In the name of Jesus.

11. Blood of Jesus, break every yoke of fruitlessness in my handiwork and marital life. In the name of Jesus.

12. As You remembered Mephibosheth and brought his wandering in Lo-debar to an end, LORD, cause all wilderness wandering in my life to expire now. In the name of Jesus.

13. By my faith and trust in the Son of God (Jesus Christ), I enter my Promised Land and enjoy the peace of the Most High God. In the name of Jesus.

14. I shall no longer walk in circles but follow the LORD on the right path. In the name of Jesus.

15. LORD, I thank You for Your answer to my prayers and the victory received. In the name of Jesus.

PRAYER 31

MY DESTINY, COME OUT OF THE VALLEY OF SUFFERING

BIBLE VERSES: Romans 8:18-23

INTRODUCTION

- Sin, as embraced by Adam and Eve, has caused all creation to fall from the peaceful and perfect state in which God made it. After Adam and Eve sinned, the human race fell under the manipulation of the elements and powers of the Devil and became subjected to bondage, frustration, and decay, so it could not fulfil its intended purpose (Romans 3:23). Idolatry, witchcraft, occultism, household wickedness, etc., took control of human destiny and continued to manipulate it to the benefit of the kingdom of darkness (Job 2:7-10).
- Cases abound in the world of people who are deformed in one aspect of their lives or the other. There are people with inherited sicknesses or

infirmities; others are barren and unfruitful, poor and wretched. The people in the world know they have to contend with these problems and will go to any extent to find solutions in line with the pattern of the world. Even where they find solutions, they are temporary or lead to another problem more difficult than the one from which they escaped.

- As believers in Christ filled with the power and fire of the Holy Spirit, we would be foolish if we fail to recognize these works as those of the Devil and his agents. The Bible tells us we should not be ignorant of the Devil's devices (2 Corinthians 2:11).

- In this prayer, it is intended that there shall be an encounter with the power of the Holy Ghost to confront and defeat those powers that are manipulating or pushing your life, as well as your destiny into the valley of bondage and suffering. It is necessary, therefore, to believe all God has promised concerning you (Isaiah 49:24, 25). By faith, receive your life and God-given destiny from the valley of suffering; take them back!

- Before you pray, you must understand your relationship with the deliverer, Jesus Christ is very important. If it is not cordial, confess any shortcomings, promise to make it right and remain strong. I prophesy to your life by the resurrection power of Jesus Christ, come out of the valley of suffering right now! In Jesus' mighty name. Amen.

PRAYER POINTS:

1. My Father and God, I bless and honour Your holy name for mercy and grace in my life.
2. Blood of Jesus Christ, LORD, cancel all my sins, errors, and omissions. In the name of Jesus.
3. Pentecostal power and fire, fall upon me now. In the name of Jesus.
4. LORD, by the blood of Jesus, break the flow of any curse of suffering that came from aggrieved ancestors into my life. In the name of Jesus.
5. Conspiracy of darkness harassing my life and destiny, scatter by the fire of God. In the name of Jesus.
6. Holy Ghost fire, consume every weapon of the household enemies to stagnate my life physically and spiritually. In the name of Jesus.
7. Demonic chain holding down my life and destiny in the valley of suffering, be broken by the fire of God. In the name of Jesus.
8. My LORD and my God, deliver me from the valley of affliction and suffering created by household enemies. In the name of Jesus.

9. Every satanic prayer against my life and family, be frustrated and nullified by the blood of Jesus. In Jesus' name.

10. Blood of Jesus, heal every infirmity in my body, soul, and spirit. In the name of Jesus.

11. Resurrection power of Jesus Christ, revive every dead organ and virtue in my life. In the name of Jesus.

12. LORD, God of Elijah, appear and schedule my destiny for immediate deliverance. In Jesus' name.

13. My destiny designed by God from the beginning, come out of the valley of suffering. In the name of Jesus.

14. My revealed destiny, hear the word of God. You will never come under affliction or suffering. In the name of Jesus.

15. LORD, I thank You for Your answer to my prayers and the deliverance received. In the name of Jesus.

PRAYER 32

ENEMIES OF MY JOY AND HAPPINESS SHALL BE DISGRACED AND SILENCED

BIBLE VERSES: *Psalm 83:15-18; Isaiah 65:13-15*

INTRODUCTION

- Enemies are people who do anything contrary or against us. They operate in the physical as well as the spiritual. In fact, the spiritual ones are the most dangerous of all; they need to be dealt with quickly and seriously.
- Happiness is the state of being joyful; emotional wellbeing; when one is glad.
- Right from the beginning of the creation, God was in the habit of doing good things for His children (Genesis 1:31).
- On the other hand, the Devil from Genesis Chapter 3 until now has been in the habit of seeking to steal,

kill, and destroy the glory and happiness of human beings, especially believers in Christ (Genesis 3:1-11; John 10:10).
- The Devil's warfare is experienced in various aspects of human endeavours: marital, fruitfulness, position, promotion, success, honour, wealth, freedom, family, and nations.
- When we become believers, there is hope and belief that all will be well. In fact, it must be well. God's plan is to visit His children or His temple regularly to bless His people. The result of God's visitation and blessing is joy and happiness.
- The Devil, demons, and his human agents will seek every possible means to reverse the blessings, joy, and happiness of the people. Look at the following incidences in the Bible to illustrate the activities of the Devil in the world:
    a) Stole the glory and happiness of Adam and Eve (Genesis 3:1-24)
    b) Stole the joy, happiness, and peace of Job (Job 1:13-22)
    c) Stole the joy, happiness, and eternity of Judas Iscariot (Matthew 27:3-5)
    d) Stole the joy and happiness of the woman with the issue of blood (Mark 5:25-34)

e) Stole the joy, happiness, and prosperity of the widow (Luke 7:11-12)

- There is, therefore, the need to rise up and fight the enemies in the strength of God. This is done by reporting them to God in prayers for God to deal with them appropriately and instantly. As you reach out to God now and bring the enemies into the court of the Most High God, Jesus Christ, the divine Advocate will arise and defend you. Jesus Christ has defeated the Devil and broken his powers at Calvary. Hence, your victory today is already settled.
- Before you begin to pray, check your life and repent of known sins. Ask the LORD to come into your life to rule and reign there forever.

PRAYER POINTS:

1. Mighty and miracle-working God, I worship You for Your presence and power in my life.
2. I plead the blood of Jesus Christ, for total cleansing and coverage. In the name of Jesus.
3. God, arise in Your power and frustrate every plan of the dark kingdom to steal my joy and happiness. In the name of Jesus.

4. Persecute the wicked in my life with Your tempest and make them unstable, O LORD. In the name of Jesus.

5. Holy Ghost fire, dry up every source of pain and suffering in my life. In the name of Jesus.

6. LORD, fill the faces of my enemies with shame and disgrace. In the name of Jesus.

7. Satanic veil of darkness covering my eyes to rob me of my blessings, be torn off. In the name of Jesus.

8. Ancestral power of my father's house withholding the keys of my progress, be dispossessed and die by fire. In the name of Jesus.

9. Satanic manipulations designed to rob me of my joy and happiness, be nullified by the blood of Jesus.

10. LORD, confound and trouble those who have put themselves under a vow to trouble me. In the name of Jesus.

11. Anywhere my glory and happiness are being held hostage, Holy Ghost, set them free. In the name of Jesus.

12. Make Your joy and happiness swallow every trial and sorrow in my life. In the name of Jesus.

13. The LORD shall paralyze and devour every devourer of my happiness. In the name of Jesus.

14. The object of my praise to You, LORD, shall be so wonderful to silence my enemies. In the name of Jesus.
15. LORD, I thank You for prompt answers to my prayers and the deliverance received. In the name of Jesus.

PRAYER 33

EVIL SOUL-TIES IN MY LIFE MUST BE BROKEN

BIBLE VERSES: *1 Samuel 18:1-4*

INTRODUCTION

- The "soul" is the individual or essential self of every human being; the spiritual or immortal aspect (element) of a person, while the word "tie" is to attach or fasten with cord; to link; to connect. Soul-tie, therefore, is the linkage or connection of an individual with another.
- A soul-tie may be good or evil. For example, the kind of soul-tie in our Bible verses between David and Jonathan was a good one. On the other hand, the connection of anyone with dead relatives or satanic personalities will naturally be an evil soul-tie. Thus, our concern today is the evil soul-tie.

- An evil soul-tie is when two or more people come together with the desire or plan to do things that are evil. By the definition, an evil soul-tie is a very bad relationship that needs to be done away with immediately when discovered.
- Evil soul-ties that are most dangerous are the ones that originate in the dream. It manifests with you seeing yourself having to do things together:
  a) Parents or friends that are dead still give instructions to their children or friends who are living or give gifts to them including money, food, etc.
  b) Having husbands or wives in the dream, sleeping with them and having children including breastfeeding or playing with babies born in the dreams
  c) Seeing strange things in dreams including:
     - Attending former schools or classes
     - Working in former places of employment
     - Still living in former residences
     - Still attending former places of worship and so on
- In spiritual terms, all the above illustrations are evil and need to be dealt with quickly. They must be

dealt with as soon as they manifest because they are signs of stagnation, limitation, retrogression, frustration, failure, confusion, sickness, and even untimely death in the life of anyone involved.

- The causes of evil soul-ties are so many but the one of satanic manipulation is when the dark kingdom investigates people's lives and resorts to the best form of evil soul-ties to torment them.

- For unbelievers, there should be no surprise because the oppression cannot find the coverage of the blood of Jesus. But for believers, it is a serious reproach. The way out is to search your life to see if there is any hidden sin, which must be confessed immediately. In addition, serious prayers must be undertaken because once the soul-tie is in place, it is very hard to break.

- If unbelievers fully surrender to the Lordship of Jesus Christ and pray fervently, using the name and blood of Jesus Christ, the evil soul-tie has no alternative than to break. As you do this now, let your faith be strong in the ability of the mighty God to break the evil soul-tie. Therefore, I prophesy that any form of evil soul-tie operating in your life shall hear the Word of God and break. In Jesus' mighty name. Amen.

PRAYER POINTS:

1. Rock of Ages, I magnify Your holy name for Your great power to break every yoke of the Enemy.
2. I plead the blood of Jesus for cleansing and coverage of myself and family. In the name of Jesus.
3. Holy Ghost thunder, break any evil soul-tie that came into my life through the covenant or curse of my ancestors, grandparents or parents. In the name of Jesus.
4. Evil soul-tie with my parents either dead or living, break and release me. In the name of Jesus.
5. Evil soul-tie with relatives or friends that are dead, break by the blood of Jesus. In Jesus' name.
6. Holy Ghost, by your fire, break evil soul-ties with household witchcraft. In the name of Jesus.
7. Evil soul-ties with former friends, girlfriends or boyfriends, break and loose your hold upon my life. In the name of Jesus.
8. Evil soul-ties with my place of birth, break and loose your hold upon my life. In the name of Jesus.
9. Evil soul-ties between me and my former places of work, worship, and residences, break and loose your hold upon my life. In the name of Jesus.

10. Evil soul-ties between me and familiar spirits, demonic and occult powers, break by the blood of Jesus. In Jesus' name.

11. Evil soul-ties between me and spiritual husbands or wives, break by the blood of Jesus. In Jesus' name.

12. All sicknesses, poverty, failure, loss or delay in my blessing as a result of evil soul-ties, merciful LORD, cancel them. In the name of Jesus.

13. Let all those who seek after my soul to destroy it, be ashamed and confounded together. In Jesus' name.

14. Rock of Ages, by Your mighty power break every evil soul-tie operating in my life. In the name of Jesus.

15. LORD, I thank You for answering my prayers and restoring all I have lost spiritually and physically due to evil soul-ties. In the name of Jesus.

PRAYER 34

BRING DISGRACE AND DESTRUCTION UPON MY ACCUSERS, O LORD!

BIBLE VERSES: Psalm 71:13 (NLT)

INTRODUCTION

"Accusers" are the people who bring the charge or charges of wrong doings against others. In the Bible, Satan is referred to as the accuser of the brethren (Revelation 12:10) together with all his human agents. They make false accusations about the brethren.

1 Kings 21:1-16 contains the story of Naboth, an innocent man who owned a vineyard close to the palace of King Ahab. Out of envy, Ahab, with the assistance of his wife Jezebel, arranged for false accusers to speak against Naboth; they murdered him and took possession of his vineyard. Invariably, every false accusation either then or now is designed to bring trouble or calamity to the victim. In the Bible verse, the psalmist recognized this and wasted no time

reporting his accusers to God to intervene before the calamity occurred. Perhaps if Naboth had taken steps to act like the psalmist in his prayers, he might have escaped the evil of Ahab's home against him. However, true to His nature, God eventually avenged the murder of Naboth upon the house of Ahab.

In praying these prayers, no time will be wasted in addressing such situations which, if not already begun, are likely to come on our Christian journey. I prophesy, therefore, that the LORD shall arise for your sake today and bring disgrace and destruction upon your accusers before they destroy you. In the mighty name of Jesus. Amen.

PRAYER POINTS:

1. Most gracious and powerful God, I bless and honour Your most holy name for what You are doing in my life. Be exalted forever. In the name of Jesus.

2. I draw from the multitude of Your mercies for my life today. In the name of Jesus.

3. I plead the blood of Jesus and cover myself, as well as all that belongs to me with the blood. In the name of Jesus.

4. Blood of Jesus, wipe out every mark of household witchcraft in my life. In the name of Jesus.

5. LORD, fill me with Your revelation power, authority, and fire for today's assignment. In the name of Jesus.

6. LORD, grant me discernment of times and judgment and make me wiser than my adversaries. In the name of Jesus.

7. Every conspiracy of Satan and his agents against my life and destiny, be scattered by the fire of God. In the name of Jesus.

8. LORD, disgrace all false accusers and cancel their accusations in my life and family. In the name of Jesus.

9. Holy Ghost thunder, break into pieces every evil mirror employed by the accusers to monitor my life. In the name of Jesus.

10. Holy Spirit, render every piece of information about me useless in the hands of my accusers. In the name of Jesus.

11. God, arise and vindicate me of every accusation put forward by my accusers. In the name of Jesus.

12. LORD, use every detail of my life and destiny to confuse and confound my accusers. In the name of Jesus.

13. I refuse to be submerged by the violent torrent of words from my accusers. In the name of Jesus.

14. I shall prevail over every accuser and their accusations. In the name of Jesus.
15. Father LORD, I thank You most sincerely for answering these prayers by Your fire. In the name of Jesus.

PRAYER 35

BREAK THE STAFF AND SCEPTER OF WICKED RULERS IN MY LIFE, O LORD!

BIBLE VERSE: Isaiah 14:5

INTRODUCTION

The "staff" is the symbol of power, while the "scepter" is the symbol of authority in the hands of rulers either just or unjust. Power is the ability to do things unhindered, while authority is the seal or force of the orders made. For our purpose here, we are concerned with the unjust rulers (oppressors). When the power and authority of the oppressors are broken in your life, it signifies the end of such evil rule.

The accounts of the Israelites in Egypt (Exodus Chapters 2 and 3) and Judah in Babylon (Isaiah Chapter 14) are clear examples of evil rule over the people of God. God is aware of what goes on in the lives of His people. When He decides to intervene and deliver them from the oppressor's rule, He breaks the power and authority or control of such rule over them.

In our present circumstances, we may or may not physically recognize evil rulers or oppressors in our society, around us or even very close to us. Their activities are usually carried out in the spirit realm and sometimes physically. They are designed to make life difficult for their victims.

As believers in Christ, however, we know God is omnipotent, omniscient, and omnipresent. He has the superlative power to deliver His people. Hence, there is a need to cry unto Him against every form of oppression in our lives. Therefore, I prophesy that the LORD shall look down from heaven, command all the evil rulers in your life to be paralyzed, their staff and scepter broken, and set you free. In Jesus' mighty name. Amen.

PRAYER POINTS:

1. Mighty and most powerful God, I thank You for Your wonderful works in my life. May Your most holy name be praised forever. In the name of Jesus.
2. I plead the blood of Jesus and cover myself and all that belongs to me with the blood. In Jesus' name.
3. Power, authority, and fire from God, come upon me now. In the name of Jesus.

4. Ancestral curse or covenant responsible for the power and authority of evil rulers in my life, be broken by the blood of Jesus. In Jesus' name.

5. Seed of oppression planted by household enemies into my life, be uprooted by the fire of God. In the name of Jesus.

6. Whatever has drawn me into the network of the oppressor against my will, Father, expose and destroy it now. In the name of Jesus.

7. Agents of oppression in my life, home or workplace, be paralyzed and die. In the name of Jesus.

8. Instruments of oppression of the evil rulers in my life and family, catch fire and burn to ashes. In the name of Jesus.

9. Spirit of discernment fall upon me now to recognize demonic environments and snares, so I can take the necessary action. In the name of Jesus.

10. God, arise in Your mighty power for my sake now. Break the staff and scepter of wicked rulers in my life and family. In the name of Jesus.

11. Holy Ghost, put my oppressors in chains and turn the tide against them. In the name of Jesus.

12. LORD, locate my life with Your multiple promotions in all areas of my calling and endeavours. In the name of Jesus.

13. From today, LORD, silence the boastful words of the evil rulers in my life. In the name of Jesus.
14. LORD, make my victory and deliverance from the evil rulers a testimony of the demonstration of Your mighty power in my life. In the name of Jesus.
15. Wonderful LORD, I thank You for Your answers to these prayers and the victory. In the name of Jesus.

PRAYER 36

EXPOSE AND FRUSTRATE THE EVIL AGENDA OF MY ADVERSARIES, O LORD!

BIBLE VERSE: *2 Kings 6:9-10*

INTRODUCTION

An "evil agenda" is a harmful plan, thought or intention of a person, group of persons or nations against another; it is designed to have bad or destructive consequences on such a person, persons or nations. Quite often, an evil agenda is the handiwork of evil people (the wicked), adversaries or enemies. It is aimed at attacking other people's existence, progress, success or peace to reverse the pattern or trend of good things in people's lives.

An evil agenda is carried out in secret outside the view or knowledge of the victims (those to be attacked). It is done this way to have the surprise effect and shock at the sudden manifestation of such plans or intentions of the attacks (Psalm 10:8-9). Because of the secrecy of an evil agenda, only the LORD, the omniscient God can expose or frustrate the plans of your enemies without the help of a traitor within the organizers of the evil agenda (Jeremiah 17:9-10; Isaiah 7:5-7).

In our Bible verse, the LORD revealed the evil agenda of the king of Syria against Israel to the prophet Elisha who, in turn, exposed it to the king of Israel and consequently, it was frustrated. Thus, it can be seen clearly that the frustration of the evil plans of the king of Syria was motivated and executed by the LORD through His prophet.

In light of the above and having regard for the prevalence of an evil agenda as one of the traits of a society with decaying moral values and an attack that leads to aborted plans, progress, success of honest people or even their premature or premeditated deaths, it is necessary in these prayers to deal with and destroy any evil agenda that may be standing against us. I prophesy, therefore, that the LORD shall arise for your sake now. He will expose and frustrate every evil agenda in your life. In Jesus' mighty name. Amen.

PRAYER POINTS:

1. Everlasting and gracious God, I bless and magnify You for what You are doing in my life. Receive all adoration and thanksgiving. In the name of Jesus.

2. I plead the precious blood of Jesus Christ for cleansing and total coverage. In the name of Jesus.
3. Holy Ghost fire, come upon me afresh now. In the name of Jesus.
4. LORD, open Your armoury and equip me with spiritual weapons for today's warfare. In the name of Jesus.
5. Spirits of revelation and discernment from the LORD fall upon me now. In the name of Jesus.
6. God, arise! Expose and frustrate every evil agenda of my adversaries. In the name of Jesus.
7. Holy Ghost thunder, scatter every conspiracy of the dark kingdom against my life. In Jesus' name.
8. LORD, blow the evil agenda of my adversaries into their own eyes. In the name of Jesus.
9. Unquenchable fire of God's anger, devour every hidden or cleverly concealed evil planner gathering against my life and family. In the name of Jesus.
10. LORD, frustrate the tokens of every liar in my life and silence them forever. In Jesus' name.
11. Every spiritual or physical robber of my well-being and glory, surrender them now and die by fire. In the name of Jesus.
12. Arrows of evil words and spells fired into my life, return to your senders. In the name of Jesus.

13. God of signs and wonders, turn every evil plan of my adversaries into a channel of outstanding miracles in my life. In the name of Jesus.

14. My star, what are you doing in the valley of suffering? Arise and shine, never to be manipulated again. In the name of Jesus.

15. LORD, I thank You for answering these prayers by fire. In the name of Jesus.

PRAYER 37

DELIVER MY FINANCES AND BARRICADE THEM FROM SATANIC ONSLAUGHT, O LORD!

BIBLE VERSE: *Jeremiah 30:16 (NKJV)*

INTRODUCTION

A "satanic onslaught" simply stated means Satan's fierce attack. When it is launched against anyone's finances, its consequences are always very disastrous. Financial sufficiency or wealth is God's will for His children (believers), especially those who seek Him (Psalm 34:10). This is necessary to guard such children against covetousness and suffering. It is also to give them the desired protection, prosperity, peace, and comfort in life.

As it is expected, Satan, who is the undisputed Enemy of all that is of God, especially God's children, will always seek to attack fiercely and destroy anything that can ensure the comfort of God's children including their finances (John

10:10). Some of the methods usually employed by Satan to attack people's finances include:

a) sin of disobedience
b) lukewarmness
c) carelessness
d) sickness or infirmity
e) manipulation (in the dream or physical)
f) unnecessary borrowing
g) unnecessary financial ties or project expenditure
h) piling up treasures on earth instead of heaven

The consequences of satanic attacks on people's finances, especially God's children have always been to lead its victims into serious financial hardship. The only potent way of escape or deliverance from fierce, satanic attacks is God's way as declared in His Word (2 Timothy 2:26 and 1 Corinthians 10:13). God's Word will expose our errors or omissions, direct our return to the path of the LORD seeking His intervention by faith and inspire us to pray for deliverance, as well as the return of all that has been taken away by the oppressor (Isaiah 49:24-25).

The following prayers provide the means by which we can ask the LORD to intervene and set our finances free from fierce satanic attacks. I prophesy, therefore, that the LORD shall be gracious and entreated by your prayers. He will fight for you, deliver you, and henceforth barricade your finances from any fierce satanic attacks. In Jesus' mighty name. Amen.

PRAYER POINTS:

1. Omnipotent God, I thank You and glorify Your most holy name for Your faithfulness in my life and family. In the name of Jesus.
2. I plead the blood of Jesus Christ and cover myself and my family by the blood. In the name of Jesus.
3. Holy Ghost, ignite my prayers with Your fire. In the name of Jesus.
4. Evil altars in my present location, be dismantled. Priest and ruler of them fall and die. In the name of Jesus.
5. Evil strongman of my father's house sitting upon my financial inheritance, be struck down by the thunder of the Holy Ghost. In the name of Jesus.
6. Every gateman or guard assigned to watch over my finances in the satanic bank, Holy Ghost thunder strike him dead. In the name of Jesus.
7. LORD, destroy every satanic manipulation of my finances in the dream and in the physical by the blood of Jesus. In the name of Jesus.
8. God, arise for my sake now and withdraw my finances from satanic bondage. Return them to me. In the name of Jesus.

9. I withdraw my wealth and prosperity from the hands of the bondwoman and her children. In the name of Jesus.

10. LORD, wipe out every form of financial dryness in my life. In the name of Jesus.

11. I pull off all garments of poverty or financial wretchedness and command them to be burnt by fire. In the name of Jesus.

12. Holy Ghost, disgrace and silence every power that wants me to pay for what I did not buy. In the name of Jesus.

13. Every satanic meeting convened to pull me down financially, be scattered by the fire of God. In the name of Jesus.

14. I shall continue to enjoy the victory, favour, good health, peace, and prosperity from the almighty God. In the name of Jesus.

15. Faithful LORD, I thank You for answering these prayers by Your fire. In the name of Jesus.

PRAYER 38

EVERY HAMAN IN MY LIFE MUST DIE

BIBLE VERSE: *Esther 7:10*

INTRODUCTION

The book of Esther in the Bible contains the fascinating story of Mordecai the Jew, his divine deliverance from the evil plot of Haman who was the enemy of the Jews, and the eventual destruction of Haman himself. Haman, a senior official in the kingdom of King Ahasuerus of Persia and Media, hated the Jews and plotted the destruction of Mordecai, as well as all the Jews in the kingdom.

The account of the great deliverance of Mordecai and the Jews was predicated on the special fasting and praying involving Esther the queen and Mordecai's niece, Mordecai himself, and all the Jews in the kingdom. God worked behind the scenes to deliver His people and promote Mordecai through the wisdom of Queen Esther, while Haman, his family, and people were destroyed.

The enmity between the Jews and the Amalekites from which tribe Haman belonged, was age-long. It went as far back as the time of the reign of King Saul when God commanded their destruction (1 Samuel Chapter 15). But the fact remains the Devil was behind Haman's actions.

As the adversary, the Devil still roams about seeking to devour the children of God (1 Peter 5:8) through his agents such as Haman and the likes. Hence, it is intended here that we will follow the example of Esther, Mordecai, and the Jews to seek the face of God to avenge us. We will call upon Him to disgrace and destroy every agent of the Devil tormenting lives and destinies. Therefore, I prophesy that every Haman in your life and destiny shall die by the very instrument of destruction prepared for you. You shall be divinely promoted. In Jesus' mighty name. Amen.

PRAYER POINTS:

1. Omnipotent, omniscient, and omnipresent God, Jehovah El-Shaddai, I worship and adore You for the opportunity to be one of Your children.

2. I plead the blood of Jesus Christ for cleansing and total coverage by the blood. In the name of Jesus.

3. Any part of my body that is caged in a demonic prison or evil altar, be released now. In the name of Jesus.

4. Every Haman in any critical department of my life, LORD, expose and destroy him. In the name of Jesus.
5. Holy Ghost, chase out by Your fire every spirit of Haman in any member of my family. In the name of Jesus.
6. Every instrument of death prepared for me by the Enemy, LORD, command Your hosts of heaven to use it for the destruction of those who prepared it. In the name of Jesus.
7. Cover not the disgrace of any destroyer in my life, O LORD. Let their disgrace be announced to the whole world. In the name of Jesus.
8. I command every evil wind blowing across my way to take reverse gear and go back to your source. In the name of Jesus.
9. Let every load of tribulation and suffering prepared for me by wicked family members be returned to their heads. In the name of Jesus.
10. LORD, bring to dead silence, every noise of the Enemy in the affairs of my life. In the name of Jesus.
11. Every evil writing or judgment standing against me in the dark kingdom, be wiped out by the blood of Jesus. In the name of Jesus.

12. With Your mighty hands, O LORD, draw my glory out of the mire (mud, slum, pit) of the world. In the name of Jesus.

13. LORD, disgrace and silence any contender in that place of Your destiny for my life. In the name of Jesus.

14. LORD, by Your mighty power, promote me beyond my greatest imagination and to the disgrace of my enemies. In the name of Jesus.

15. LORD, I thank You for answering these prayers by Your fire. In the name of Jesus.

PRAYER 39

SPOIL MY SPOILERS, O LORD

BIBLE VERSE: *Proverbs 22:23*

INTRODUCTION

Plunder, ruin, deprive are some of the words used in various Bible translations for the word "spoil." To an extent, they explain what the word "spoil" means. Spoilers will always oppress others using violent attacks – spiritual or physical – on the person or properties of their victims. After which, they are left devastated.

Although spoilers more often than not find it convenient to attack the poor, the fact remains that spoilers are found in every sphere of life or society. The activities of spoilers lead them to oppress fellow human beings and bring affliction, torment, and sorrow upon their victims. God finds this highly detestable.

Believers in Christ know very well that spoilers are enemies, and they may be in the household, environment, workplace, society or even in the church. They know also that the

LORD is the great deliverer to whom they must reach out for deliverance when the operation of the spoilers is noticed. Hence, potent prayers will be made here to disgrace all spoilers from our lives. I prophesy that the LORD shall rise, plead your cause, and spoil all those who spoil you. In the mighty name of Jesus Christ.

PRAYER POINTS:

1. Wonderful Father, I worship and adore You for what You are set to do once again in my life.
2. I plead the blood of Jesus Christ for cleansing and total coverage of myself. In the name of Jesus.
3. Holy Spirit, fill my prayers today with Your fire. In the name of Jesus.
4. Every satanic embargo on my life, destiny, and goodness, LORD, dismantle. In the name of Jesus.
5. LORD, turn every habitation of the wicked built against my life into desolation. In the name of Jesus.
6. Spoilers in my life, your end has come. Receive the judgment of double destruction. In the name of Jesus.
7. Every rage of the Enemy against the manifestation of my turnaround miracle, be disgraced and silenced. In the name of Jesus.

8. LORD, repair and restore every good thing, which the spoiler has destroyed in my life and destiny. In the name of Jesus.

9. Whatsoever is responsible for sorrow and sadness in my life, home, etc., LORD, uproot it by Your fire. In the name of Jesus.

10. LORD, frustrate all efforts of the dark kingdom to hinder God's plan and agenda for my life. In the name of Jesus.

11. LORD, increase every instrument or object of joy, happiness, and peace in my life and home. In the name of Jesus.

12. Henceforth, I shall not fall into the snare of the fowler or serve my enemies. In the name of Jesus.

13. On my journey of life, LORD, let Your secret place be my dwelling place. In the name of Jesus.

14. I shall always overcome my enemies' attacks, and they shall bow to my authority. In the name of Jesus.

15. LORD, I thank You for answering these prayers and for the deliverance received. In the name of Jesus.

PRAYER 40

SETTLE ME, O LORD!

BIBLE VERSE: 1 Peter 5:10

INTRODUCTION

"To settle" in the spiritual context simply means "to bring a person into the unique position of complete or full rest." For the LORD to settle you, therefore, is for Him to do all that is necessary for you to attain all-round prosperity, peace, and rest.

The LORD made human beings for His praise (Jeremiah 13:11). The heavenly Father desires all His children to live and rest in prosperity and perfect peace (Isaiah 26:3). The disobedience of our first parent, Adam and Eve (Genesis 3:11) thwarted God's plan and glory in human lives. From that point and until now, human beings became poor and have to struggle for virtually everything. Such struggles will always be monitored by the Devil and his agents to make sure they go on without end. The coming of Jesus Christ into the world brought the way and opportunity for restoration to human beings. It remains, however, for human beings to accept the redemptive work of Jesus Christ by believing and accepting Him as Saviour and LORD to find the desired rest.

Thus, "Settle me, O LORD" has been chosen from the list of what God will do in 1 Peter 5:10 as the focus of our prayers because of its far-reaching effects on human lives. As you cry unto the LORD in these prayers, I prophesy that the LORD shall do all that is necessary to make you perfect, establish, strengthen, and settle you. In Jesus' mighty name. Amen.

PRAYER POINTS:

1. Gracious and merciful Father, I give You honour and adoration for Your mighty and wonderful works in my life. May Your holy name be praised forever. In the name of Jesus.

2. I plead the blood of Jesus Christ and cover myself and all that belongs to me with the precious blood. In the name of Jesus.

3. Power that quenches the spiritual fire in me, be exposed and consumed out of my life by the fire of God. In the name of Jesus.

4. Holy Ghost, rekindle Your fire in me for these prayers. In the name of Jesus.

5. Whatever is in my hands or life that is hindering my progress unto perfection, Holy Ghost, chase it out by Your fire. In the name of Jesus.

6. God, arise and uproot everything You have not planted in the heavenlies that is working against my life. In the name of Jesus.

7. The battle that pursued me from birth, loose your hold over my life and die! In the name of Jesus.

8. Every affliction projected against my destiny by wicked household enemies, be frustrated now! In the name of Jesus.

9. LORD, deliver me from hearing strange voices that are capable of leading me astray. In the name of Jesus.

10. All those that are tormenting and oppressing my life, O LORD, turn their table against them. In the name of Jesus.

11. Holy Spirit, arrest and unseat any power that is sitting on the glory of God for my life. In the name of Jesus.

12. LORD, open the doors of great opportunities and prosperity unto me and my family. In the name of Jesus.

13. With all that makes You extraordinary and powerful, O God, make me perfect, establish, strengthen, and settle me now. In the name of Jesus.

14. I receive the power to move from strength to strength and unto perfection now. In the name of Jesus.
15. LORD, I thank You for answering these prayers by fire. In the name of Jesus.

PRAYER 41

BREAK IN PIECES THE GATES OF BRASS BEFORE ME, O LORD!

BIBLE VERSE: Isaiah 45:2

INTRODUCTION

Gates of brass are hard, iron-like structures or barriers designed to hinder or make easy passage impossible. Spiritually, they are hindrances to success or breakthrough. Therefore, when the LORD breaks the gates of brass into pieces, it means His removal of every hindrance or obstacle to physical and spiritual progress, success or breakthrough.

In the beginning, when God formed man and put him in the garden He planted, He did not think of any form of stagnation but commanded abundance and progress unto the man. Shortly after, Satan appeared on the scene and set stagnation, limitation, and frustration into the life of the man and, by extension, the entire human race. One of the works of Satan and, indeed, his kingdom of darkness, is to do everything possible to use iron-like objects to limit, stagnate, and hinder anyone who desires to do God's will or is chosen to be used by God.

Before the Servant (the Messiah) was born, God had chosen Him to bring the light of the gospel (the message of salvation) to the world (Acts 13:47). Thus, God had to deal with the plan of Satan to hinder by removing every obstacle preventing the work of the Messiah. The same thing He did for the Servant (the Messiah), God will do for all believers in Him – those that are commissioned to work for Him.

In recognition of the need for God's intervention in our capacity to work for Him, these prayers ask the LORD to break into pieces the gates of brass before us. I prophesy, therefore, that the LORD shall arise in His might and power, not only to break into pieces the gates of brass before you but also to cut through the bars of iron. In Jesus' mighty name. Amen.

PRAYER POINTS:

1. Omnipotent and ever faithful Father, I give You glory, honour, and adoration for Your mighty work in my life and family. May Your holy name be praised for ever. In the name of Jesus.

2. I plead the blood of Jesus Christ and cover myself and all that belongs to me with His blood. In the name of Jesus.

3. Holy Ghost, come upon me now and fill me with fresh fire for today's assignment.

4. Any problem that entered my life in the womb and continues to trouble me, blood of Jesus flush it out now. In the name of Jesus.

5. Holy Ghost, destroy every satanic power assigned to prolong my problem. In the name of Jesus.

6. Fire of God, consume the environmental powers assigned to monitor my life and block my breakthroughs. In the name of Jesus.

7. Gates of brass and iron standing as obstacles to my usefulness to God, break into pieces now! In the name of Jesus.

8. Any organ or material taken from my body for any form of sacrifice on evil altars, I withdraw you by fire. In the name of Jesus.

9. Power of resurrection, bring to life every organ of my body damaged by sickness or disease. In the name of Jesus.

10. Holy Ghost thunder, scatter and silence forever, every gathering of household witches and wizards in my family. In the name of Jesus.

11. Evil loads designed by the Enemy to weigh me down on my Christian journey, LORD, shake them out of my life by Your fire. In the name of Jesus

12. Whatever You led me to gather, O LORD, shall never be scattered by evil powers. In the name of Jesus.
13. Holy Spirit, be my instructor, helper, strength, and comforter in my God-given assignment. In the name of Jesus.
14. Anointing for success and good finishing, fall upon me now. In the name of Jesus.
15. LORD, I thank You for Your answers to these prayers. In the name of Jesus.

PRAYER 42

DESTROYING THE DEVOURERS OF MY HARVEST

BIBLE VERSE: Judges 6:1-10

INTRODUCTION

"Devourers" are destroying agents that leave the object(s) of attack or victims in a devastating state after their attack. "Harvest" is the season for gathering crops. "Devourers of the harvest," therefore, are agents of mass destruction of resources and, clearly, enemies of progress. Devourers can be spirit beings, human beings, beasts, birds or insects and the object of their attack can be the finances, wealth, health, business, work, possessions, families or thoughts of their victims.

Devourers, being agents of mass destruction, can only be instruments in the hands of the Devil to torment his victims. As expected, believers (Christians) are not exempt from the devourers of the harvest. It can be the result of the decision of the dark kingdom, which is allowed by God for a reason.

On the other hand, as illustrated in the Bible verse, when believers deviate from the profession of obedience to God's laws and embark on the course of sin, God may respond by disciplining them via the hands of the devourers. Devourers will be allowed to attack and make a clean sweep of what amounts to be the object of such disobedience or pride.

Whatever may be the reason behind our present situation, like the Israelites in the Bible verse, we must arise to cry unto God in repentance. By the intervention of heaven, the devourers of our harvest shall be destroyed. The Bible says in Psalm 145:8, 9: "The Lord is gracious and full of compassion, slow to anger, and of great mercy…and his tender mercies are over all his works." The following prayers provide the opportunity to deal with the devourers of our harvest and obtain the desired victory. Therefore, I prophesy that everything standing as a devourer in your harvest shall be consumed by the fire of God for you to possess your possessions. In Jesus' mighty name. Amen.

PRAYER POINTS:

1. Gracious and merciful God, I bless and magnify Your most holy name for Your grace upon me.
2. I plead the blood of Jesus Christ for cleansing and coverage. In the name of Jesus.
3. LORD, clothe me with Your garment of fire for effective assignments today. In the name of Jesus.

4. Any covenant or agreement I have entered unconsciously that is now working against my success, be broken and nullified by the blood of Jesus Christ. In Jesus' name.

5. Lord, close forever every access door to the devourers in my life. In the name of Jesus.

6. Let the cloud blocking the sunlight of my glory and breakthrough be dispersed. In the name of Jesus.

7. Every decision or judgment taken in the kingdom of darkness against my prosperity, be nullified by the blood of Jesus. In Jesus' name.

8. Devouring powers in the foundation of my life and business, die! In the name of Jesus.

9. I withdraw by fire all my finances siphoned away through demonic manipulation and deceit. In the name of Jesus.

10. Any project or action that will lead me into financial embarrassment, LORD, keep me out of it. In the name of Jesus.

11. All good harvests in my life devoured by devourers, O LORD, restore them in full. In the name of Jesus.

12. LORD, release Your fresh liquid fire upon all the enemies of my blessings. In the name of Jesus.

13. I refuse to cooperate with anything evil that will truncate God's plan and purpose for my life. In the name of Jesus.

14. LORD, bring me into favour with all those who will decide my advancement. In the name of Jesus.
15. LORD, I thank You for answering these prayers and the divine favour received. In the name of Jesus.

PRAYER 43

DISGRACE THE EVIL CONTENDERS OF MY DESTINY

BIBLE VERSE: Genesis 50:20

INTRODUCTION

"Evil contenders" are those agents of the kingdom of darkness operating evil, spiritual devices to monitor the affairs of people's lives negatively. They strive relentlessly to block the goodness of God in the lives of their victims. To pray that the LORD disgrace evil contenders of one's destiny, therefore, is for their plans and activities to be frustrated and all devices destroyed. Hence, such evil contenders will be put to total disgrace.

The example in our Bible verse and many more in the Bible are clear testimonies to the fact that evil contenders abound, not only in the world but also around us, even among family members. Jesus Christ, quoting the prophet Micah (Micah 7:6) said, "And a man's foes shall be they of his own household" (Matthew 10:36).

The polygamous, cultural, and religious backgrounds of families largely contribute to the emergence of evil contenders. More often, the evil contender will begin the operation against the victim from the time of birth and continue until death. Believers in Christ may be ignorant of the source of affliction in their lives more so when such affliction comes from within the family. They, no doubt, are not left without potent weapons to fight spiritual warfare. These include fasting and praying in the name of Jesus, standing in faith on God's Word to resist every contrary move and invoking the blood of Jesus Christ to counteract every evil flow, among others.

Through prayers accompanied by fasting, you can deal with every evil contender in your life. I prophesy, therefore, that the Most High God shall arise, frustrate every plan, agenda, and programme of evil contenders in your life and bring them into open disgrace. In Jesus' mighty name. Amen.

PRAYER POINTS:

1. Almighty Father, I worship and honour You for all You have done and continue to do in my life.
2. I plead the blood of Jesus Christ for cleansing and total coverage. In the name of Jesus.
3. Holy Spirit, help my infirmity to be able to pray effectively now. In the name of Jesus.

4. Blood of Jesus, nullify every evil mark or identity placed upon me by the Enemy to facilitate his work in my life. In the name of Jesus.

5. Whatsoever platform the evil contenders are standing upon to fight my star and destiny, dismantle it, O LORD. In the name of Jesus.

6. Holy Ghost thunder, break to pieces and burn with Your fire all instruments and devices that evil contenders are using to monitor my life and destiny. In the name of Jesus.

7. Evil contenders of my good dream and destiny from my father's house, be exposed, disgraced, and silenced forever. In the name of Jesus.

8. According to Your Word, O LORD, contend with all evil contenders in my life and destiny. Fight for me and make me hold my peace. In the name of Jesus.

9. God, destroy every destroyer of life and property in my life and make them fall by their own counsels. Cast their ashes into the pit they have made. In the name of Jesus.

10. LORD, by the power of Your resurrection, lift me up and deliver me from every pit of despair and disappointment. In the name of Jesus.

11. Clothe all my adversaries with the garment of shame, O LORD, and let them cover themselves with their confusion. In the name of Jesus.

12. As You magnified Joseph in the sight of the evil contenders of his father's house, LORD, magnify me in the sight of all contenders in my life and destiny. In the name of Jesus.

13. As the sun, moon, and stars cannot be hindered from their glorious function, LORD, let my star and destiny receive new strength and shine. In the name of Jesus.

14. By Your mighty hands, O LORD, promote me beyond my highest imagination and to the shame of all evil contenders. In the name of Jesus.

15. Wonderful LORD, I thank You, once again, for answering these prayers by Your fire. In the name of Jesus.

PRAYER 44

ROLL AWAY EVERY OBJECT OF HINDRANCE, LIMITATION, AND | STAGNATION IN MY LIFE, O LORD!

BIBLE VERSE: *Matthew 28:2*

INTRODUCTION

Objects of hindrance, limitation, and stagnation, wherever they exist, are the things designed or put in place to make freedom or progress impossible. They are weapons in the hands of the Enemy to frustrate the efforts of their victims.

The story in the Bible of the death and resurrection of Jesus Christ (Matthew 27:57, 28:6) is a clear testimony of the power of God to deliver us, even in hopeless situations. The enemies of Jesus Christ not only opposed Him while alive but also attempted to frustrate any form of miracle that could accompany His death.

In their physical and spiritual journey of life, believers in Christ have to seriously contend with Satan, his agents and the host of the dark kingdom whose assignments are to hinder, limit or stagnate believers. In the case of Jesus Christ, God put all His enemies to shame and disgrace by the miraculous resurrection of Jesus Christ.

As you call on God Almighty in the following prayers, He will surely hearken unto you and do the same in your life. Therefore, I prophesy that the Almighty God, the most powerful and awesome, shall send an earthquake and command His angels from heaven to roll away every stone of hindrance, limitation, and stagnation in your life. In Jesus' mighty name. Amen.

PRAYER POINTS:

1. Everlasting and gracious Father, I bless and honour You for what You are doing in my life. May Your most holy name be praised forever. In the name of Jesus.

2. I plead the blood of Jesus Christ and cover myself and all that belongs to me with the blood. In the name of Jesus.

3. By Your mercy, O LORD, destroy every legal ground on which Satan and his agents are standing on to oppress my life. In the name of Jesus.

4. I dismantle and destroy whatever the Enemy has done to hinder my progress. In the name of Jesus.

5. LORD, scatter every conspiracy of the dark kingdom to keep me in perpetual bondage. In the name of Jesus.

6. Holy Ghost, tear off and burn by Your fire every garment of shame, disgrace, and death the Enemy has designed for my life. In the name of Jesus.

7. LORD, send Your great earthquake and angels from heaven and roll away every stone of hindrance, limitation, and stagnation in my life. In the name of Jesus.

8. By the power of Your resurrection, O LORD, put every evil agitator in my life into permanent frustration and silence. In the name of Jesus.

9. By the power of the resurrection of Jesus Christ, every good thing in my life that has died, come alive now. In the name of Jesus.

10. LORD, remove every obstacle placed in my way to prevent my breakthrough and success. In the name of Jesus.

11. Just as the grave and its cover stone could not detain Jesus' glory, no satanic power shall be able to hold down my miracle and glory. In the name of Jesus.

12. LORD, make my life and destiny too hot for the Enemy to handle or manipulate. In the name of Jesus.
13. By the power of the resurrection of Jesus Christ that put the Devil to shame, O LORD, put him and his agents to shame and disgrace in my life. In the name of Jesus.
14. LORD, cause the star of my glory to shine perpetually. In the name of Jesus.
15. LORD, I thank You for answering these prayers by Your fire. In the name of Jesus.

PRAYER 45

BRING ME OUT OF EVERY HUMILIATION OF MAN, O LORD!

BIBLE VERSE: Isaiah 54:4 (a)-(d)

INTRODUCTION

To "bring out" is to liberate, deliver or set free, while "humiliation" is to feel ashamed or disgraced. To pray that the LORD brings us out of every humiliation of man is to ask the LORD to liberate, deliver or set us free from every shameful or disgraceful situation brought about by the activities of evil people in our lives.

In the prophecy of Isaiah Chapter 54, we see that barrenness was chosen to illustrate the point of God's plan of intervention in the humiliation or shame of Judah and Jerusalem. Barrenness (childlessness or fruitlessness) are still prominent and serious causes of humiliation and shame in marriages (Hannah in 1 Samuel 1:6). Other reasons include sin, sickness or deformity, poverty, failure, limitation and stagnation, standing on the truth, various kinds of domination, etc. All of these are prone to bring about stigmatization by the society, especially our adversaries.

The Devil in his function as a thief, murderer, and destroyer (John 10:10) will always possess and manipulate human agents to humiliate people unjustifiably and so bring defeat and problems into the lives of others. However, the coming of Jesus Christ, the Son of God into the world was to destroy the works of the Devil (1 John 3:8). Therefore, the LORD provides a good opportunity for anyone who cries to Him to deal with every work of the Devil and darkness.

The recognition of this truth and the promise of deliverance informed the following prayers, so we can serve God without fear, in holiness and righteousness before him, all the days of our lives (Luke 1:74-75). I prophesy, therefore, that the LORD shall arise now, contend with evil people in your life and bring you out of all the humiliation of man. In Jesus' mighty name. Amen.

PRAYER POINTS:

1. Merciful and gracious God, I give You glory and honour for Your love and grace in my life.
2. I plead the blood of Jesus Christ and cover myself and all that belongs to me with the blood. In the name of Jesus.

3. Holy Ghost, purify and clothe me with Your fire. In the name of Jesus.

4. Any flow of the Adamic nature into my life, blood of Jesus wash it away. In the name of Jesus.

5. Holy Ghost, dismantle by Your fire every satanic stronghold in my life. In the name of Jesus.

6. Garments of humiliation, reproach, and shame in my life, be torn off and consumed by fire. In the name of Jesus.

7. Garments of sorrow, sickness, and untimely death in my life, be torn off and burnt into ashes. In the name of Jesus.

8. Holy Ghost thunder, scatter every gathering and plan of the enemies to humiliate my life. In the name of Jesus.

9. I nullify every satanic agenda and calendar in my life. In the name of Jesus.

10. The LORD that frustrates the tokens of the liars, frustrate the tokens of humiliating liars in my life. In the name of Jesus.

11. Whatever has been done by anybody to hinder my progress and greatness spiritually and physically, LORD, command it to give way now. In the name of Jesus.

12. LORD, by Your mighty hand, bring me out and deliver me from every form of humiliation,

reproach, and disgrace of household enemies. In the name of Jesus.

13. LORD, turn the humiliation and reproach of my enemies into stepping stones for my promotion. In the name of Jesus.

14. With their hands on their mouths in disgrace, all my adversaries shall behold the glory of God in my life and be silenced forever. In the name of Jesus.

15. Wonderful LORD, I thank You for answering these prayers by Your fire. In the name of Jesus.

PRAYER 46

BREAK THE CURSE OF FAILURE IN MY EARNEST EXPECTATION IN YOU, O LORD!

BIBLE VERSES: Philippians 1:20; Romans 8:19 (CSBV)

INTRODUCTION

By "earnest expectation" means the eager hope of success in reaching the goal set by Jesus Christ for every believer in Him. This goal is for them to honour Christ with their lives. Thus, their main focus, desire, and hope in life is to become sons and daughters of God (John 1:12) in honour of Jesus Christ. In the same vein, they are to become instruments for bringing others to follow Him as well.

While the heathens (unbelievers) desire, focus on or struggle with mundane (earthly) things, the true believer's main desire, focus or struggle must be spiritual (heavenly) (Colossians 3:2). When a believer who is expected to be spiritually inclined (alert) and progressing to perfection

(Matthew 5:48) continues to focus more on earthly things, distractions come and there is inherent failure. Even success in physical efforts can be hindered because the spiritual controls the physical.

It is an undeniable fact that the main reason for the manifestation of the serpent (the Devil) (Genesis 3:1) was to put in place the curse of failure in human lives. It is also gratifying that through the love of God (John 3:16), Jesus Christ came and His manifestation also destroyed the works of the Devil (1 John 3:8).

The failure of some believers to seize the opportunity for full deliverance provided by Jesus Christ is the reason for the prevailing failure and disgrace they experience through their ignorance, errors, omissions, and faithlessness. Hence, these prayers will provide unique opportunities for us to get rid of our shortcomings, break the curse of failure and be established firmly by the LORD on the way to success spiritually and physically. I prophesy, therefore, that the LORD shall arise. By His mighty hand and the blood of Jesus Christ, He will break every curse of failure in our earnest expectation to honour Him with our lives. In Jesus' mighty name. Amen.

PRAYER POINTS:

1. Mighty and gracious God, I bless and honour You for who You are. Receive all praise and adoration. In the name of Jesus.

2. I plead the blood of Jesus Christ for cleansing and coverage. In the name of Jesus.

3. Holy Ghost, fill my prayers with Your fire. In the name of Jesus.

4. Powers from my foundation assigned to make shipwreck of my journey in life, die by the fire of God! In the name of Jesus.

5. Generational curse of failure operating in my life and family, break by the blood of Jesus. In Jesus' name.

6. Arrow of failure fired into my life in the physical and in the dream, come out! Go back to your sender and backfire. In the name of Jesus.

7. Evil spiritual consultants hired against my life, fall into your own snare of shame and destruction. In the name of Jesus.

8. Any programme of shame or disgrace on my Christian journey, be purged by the blood of Jesus. In Jesus' name.

9. Holy Ghost fire, dismantle every hindrance or embargo built by the dark kingdom against my manifestation as God's Son. In the name of Jesus.

10. My Father, my Father, my Father, make haste to help me and be pleased to deliver me. In the name of Jesus.
11. Let Your truth continually preserve me, O LORD. In the name of Jesus.
12. Organs of my body receive fresh fire and begin to honour and glorify Jesus Christ. In Jesus' name.
13. LORD, release Your uncommon blessings on my earnest expectation and hope in You. In the name of Jesus.
14. On my Christian journey, I refuse to be a failure. In the name of Jesus.
15. LORD, I thank You for Your prompt answer to these prayers. In the name of Jesus.

PRAYER 47

FRUSTRATING SATANIC ARROWS

BIBLE VERSES: *Ephesians 6:10-18*

INTRODUCTION

A bow and arrow are components of a deadly weapon of war.

A physical arrow, when released or fired from the bow by an expert archer, is aimed at a target on the victim. When the target is achieved, it is capable of entering the body of the victim like a bullet. With a poisonous head touching the body of the victim, it can result in serious wounding or death. Spiritual arrows or satanic arrows operate in the same way, but they cannot be seen physically. This makes it more dangerous and very deadly.

The victim cannot know when satanic arrows are fired by the Enemy but can only feel the impact when the arrow hits its target on any part of the body. Like the physical arrow, the same end is achieved, that is, the victim is seriously wounded or dead. Spiritual arrows are the regular weapons used by the dark kingdom to execute vengeance on people or to fight back when provoked.

However, it is very comforting to know that believers have a lot of spiritual weapons to counter the arrows from the Enemy or dark kingdom. These include the whole armour of God (Ephesians 6:12) and, in particular, the shield of faith (Ephesians 6:16), the name and blood of Jesus (John 14:14; Revelations 12:11) among others. When the armour is in place in the believer's life there is nothing to fear.

With the help of the Holy Spirit, the movement of satanic arrows can be discerned. When the right weapon of prayer is released, the arrow from the satanic and dark kingdom is frustrated and sent back to the source. I prophesy, therefore, that every satanic arrow fired into your life shall be frustrated. In Jesus' mighty name. Amen.

PRAYER POINTS:

1. Wonderful Jesus, I worship You for the power and potency that is in Your name and blood.
2. I plead the blood of Jesus for total cleansing and coverage. In the name of Jesus.
3. I stand against any power that is ready to resist me and my prayers. In the name of Jesus.
4. Holy Ghost fire, break and melt all satanic resistance to my prayers. In the name of Jesus.

5. Every conspiracy of the dark kingdom against my life, scatter by the thunder of God. In the name of Jesus.

6. Every satanic arrow fired into my life in the dream, I command you to come out and return to your sender. In the name of Jesus.

7. Every seed of sickness planted into my life through witchcraft manipulation in the dream, be uprooted and consumed by the fire of God. In the name of Jesus.

8. Unseen powers using evil arrows to trouble my life, be exposed and destroyed by the fire of God. In the name of Jesus.

9. LORD, render every satanic move or plan against my life useless. In the name of Jesus.

10. Let them that seek after my soul to destroy it be confounded and put to shame. In the name of Jesus.

11. Break the arm of the wicked and the evil ones raised against my life. In the name of Jesus.

12. LORD, release Your weapon of war and destroy every satanic instrument or weapon fashioned against me. In the name of Jesus.

13. LORD, build Your wall of fire around me and all that belongs to me. In the name of Jesus.

14. Paralyze every satanic power in my life and release Your divine protection upon me, O LORD. In the name of Jesus.
15. LORD, I thank You for answering my prayers and putting the Enemy into permanent silence. In the name of Jesus.

PRAYER 48

PULLING DOWN THE HABITATION OF THE WICKED

BIBLE VERSES: 2 Corinthians 10:3-6; Ephesians 6:10-18

INTRODUCTION

A "habitation" is a place to live in, while "the wicked" refers to the evil, morally bad people. Therefore, the "habitation of the wicked" means the living place of the evil ones. The habitation of the wicked exists in various degrees, dimensions, and places. Although it cannot be seen physically, its location can be around people, homes, families, communities, cities, and nations all over the world.

The primary purpose of its existence, wherever the location, is to oppose or frustrate all that is God's or godly destinies for mankind. Once a person with good prospects in life is unlucky to be born into this location, the tendency is for him/her to live an entire life of misery. The same fate can befall families, communities, cities, and countries where the habitation of the wicked exists.

It is quite unfortunate that believers (Christians) through sheer ignorance or pride share in the manipulations and misfortunes that are perpetrated in the habitation of the wicked around them. Instead of using the spiritual weapons of prayer to receive immediate deliverance, they rationalize God's Word and maintain that being saved, they are untouchable. However, in Ephesians 6:18, we see that part of our armour is praying always with all prayer and supplication in the Spirit. In 2 Corinthians 10:4, God's Word says, "For the weapons of our warfare are not carnal, but mighty through God to the pulling down of strongholds." Christians are expected to pull down strongholds wherever they are established.

In spiritual warfare such as this, we must release God's potent weapons against the dark kingdoms of the world to wrest our glory from them and effect our total deliverance. I prophesy, therefore, every habitation of the wicked built around you shall be destroyed and your glory released to you by fire. In the mighty name of Jesus. Amen.

PRAYER POINTS:

1. Rock of Ages, I bless and honour You for Your awesome power to breakdown strongholds.
2. I plead the blood of Jesus for cleansing and total coverage. In the name of Jesus.

3. Holy Ghost fire, incubate me for this great assignment. In the name of Jesus.

4. By the fire of God, I pull down and destroy every platform the wicked ones are standing on to fight me. In the name of Jesus.

5. All access doors to the Enemy in my life, LORD, close them down permanently. In the name of Jesus.

6. I command every mountain of adversity in my life and destiny to move and sink into the ocean of forgetfulness. In the name of Jesus.

7. Powers of darkness on evil assignment in my life, destroy yourselves. In the name of Jesus.

8. By Your mighty hands, O LORD, draw me out of every pit of despair and frustration. In the name of Jesus.

9. I lay hold on the weapons of my warfare and pull down every habitation of the wicked built around my life. In the name of Jesus.

10. I receive the sword of fire and cut down to the roots every satanic tree serving as the habitation of the wicked in my environment. In the name of Jesus.

11. I break the jaws of godless oppressors and my soul is plucked out of their mouths. In the name of Jesus.

12. Clothe all my adversaries with the garment of shame, O LORD. Cover them with confusion as with a mantle. In the name of Jesus.

13. Powers of darkness sitting on the glory of my life, be unseated and chased out. In the name of Jesus.
14. All the goodness of my life in the hands of household witchcraft, I repossess them by the fire of God. In the name of Jesus.
15. LORD, I thank You for answering these prayers by Your fire. In the name of Jesus.

PRAYER 49

HIDE ME FROM THE SCOURGE OF THE TONGUE, O LORD

BIBLE VERSE: *Job 5: 21*

INTRODUCTION:

The tongue is relatively a small member of human body, lying between the upper and lower jaws in the mouth. With the tongue, every human being is able to speak or communicate audibly. To scourge is to whip, flog or cause suffering. Scourge of the tongue, therefore, is to whip, flog or cause suffering to another person with the tongue. When one prays to be hidden from the scourge of tongue, it is for such a person to be protected from the suffering that comes through the use of tongues.

In the book of James chapter three, the tongue is referred to, among other things, as "a little member and boasts great things…, a fire…, a world of iniquity." (vv.5-6). James further descried the tongue as "an unruly evil, full of deadly poison." (v. 8). Hardly can anybody imagine the power of the spoken words from the tongue until the impact of what is spoken is evaluated (Prov.18:21). However, when the tongue is used to scourge anyone, the consequence or results of such action clearly reveals its damaging effect which eventually leaves its victim in one kind of suffering or another.

In the sins of backbiting, slander or defamation of character, the tongue plays the prominent role and those that engage in its use are set to scourge (or fight) with the tongue. David, in his days, experienced the evil that is in the scourge of tongue (2Sam.16:5-8) and was confident on the ability of God to fulfil His promise of hiding him from it (Ps.31:20b). Eliphaz, one of Job's friends also re-echoed this truth of God's promise in the.

Even though believers are admonished to avoid negative use of the tongues, there is need for protection from the scourge of the tongue coming from the evil people of the world. Hence, these prayers to God are to claim the fulfillment of His promise of hiding us from the scourge of tongues. I prophesy, therefore, that the Almighty God shall not only hide you from the scourge of the tongue but also expose and disgrace every perpetrator of this evil in your life, in Jesus mighty name, Amen.

PRAYER POINTS:

1. Heavenly Father, I worship and adore You for Your grace, mercy and peace in my life.
2. I plead the blood of Jesus Christ for cleansing and total coverage, in the name of Jesus.
3. Holy Spirit, help me to make the right impact in my prayers now, in the name of Jesus.
4. Fire of God, quench every rage of ancestral power against my being born again, in the name of Jesus.
5. Fire of God, uproot every seed of hatred sown into my life by household enemies, in the name of Jesus.
6. Whatever has been spoken into the wind against my life and destiny, be cast down, and cancelled by the blood of Jesus, in the name of Jesus.
7. Any power that has made a covenant with the sand, the water and the wind against my destiny, receive the harvest of break down and frustration, in the name of Jesus.
8. The Scriptures say that every causeless curse cannot stand, therefore, blood of Jesus, break any curse placed upon me by the wicked, in the name of Jesus.
9. Holy Ghost, silence all boastful powers delegated against my life, in the name of Jesus.

10. According to Your Word, O LORD, frustrate the token of liars in my life and turn their wisdom into foolishness, in the name of Jesus.

11. LORD, cast down every imagination and high thing that exalts itself against the knowledge of God in my life, in the name of Jesus.

12. From now, the voice of the enemy shall not prevail over me or my destiny, in the name of Jesus.

13. According to Your promise, O LORD, hide me from the scourge of the tongue, in the name of Jesus.

14. In Your power, O God, it me now with Your uncommon blessings, in the name of Jesus.

15. LORD, I thank You for Your answers to my payers, in the name of Jesus.

PRAYER 50

MAKE ME INTO A NEW SHARP INSTRUMENT FOR YOUR SERVICE, O LORD

BIBLE VERSES: Isaiah 41:15-16

INTRODUCTION

A new, sharp instrument for the LORD's service refers to a new invention of God designed in line with His plan for the liberation of mankind and the reconciliation of the world.

God the Creator (Isaiah 40:28) and the Potter (Jeremiah 18:6) possesses the absolute wisdom and capacity to fashion and make an object that will enhance His purpose for mankind and the world. God said, "I looked for someone to defend the city and to protect it from my anger, as well as stop me from destroying it. But I found no one" (Ezekiel 22:30, CEV). It is clear from God's Word there is an urgent need for a space to be filled by worthy and dependable human beings in the agenda of God for the world.

In these evil times, new, sharp instruments are required to contend with the powers of the dark kingdom of the world. They are needed to stand in the gap for God's mercy to be poured out for the salvation of the world through the precious blood of Jesus Christ. For one of the beneficiaries of God's purpose in the world to be made into a useful part of the means of fulfilling His purpose is quite appealing.

It is very important for the believer to reach out to God in prayer, to make him/her into a sharp instrument or to be renewed for divine service. I prophesy, therefore, that the Creator of heaven and earth shall perform His wonderful operation upon you and turn you into His new, sharp instrument of service. In Jesus' mighty name. Amen.

PRAYER POINTS:

1. Heavenly Father, I bless Your most holy name for making me fearfully and wonderfully.
2. By Your mercy, O LORD, blot out all my shortcomings by the blood of Jesus Christ and remember my sins no more. In the name of Jesus.
3. LORD, purify my life with Your fire. In the name of Jesus.
4. LORD, clothe me with the garment of Your power and fire to contend with and defeat the raging forces of darkness. In the name of Jesus.

5. LORD, bring down the noise of strangers in my life and silence them forever. In the name of Jesus.
6. All those things that are fighting Your good virtues in me, LORD, chase them out by Your fire. In the name of Jesus.
7. Every hindrance or delay assigned against my progress, be dismantled by fire. In the name of Jesus.
8. By Your mighty hands, O LORD, draw me out of the miry waters of life, in the name of Jesus.
9. LORD, make me into a new sharp instrument for Your service. In the name of Jesus.
10. Anywhere my present efforts at serving You fall short of Your expectation and approval, LORD, correct me in Your love. In the name of Jesus.
11. Every battle that comes my way as a result of my willingness and readiness to serve You, LORD, release Your judgment upon it. In the name of Jesus.
12. I shall not be a wrong or misfired weapon in my life and service. In the name of Jesus.
13. LORD, renew Your covenant of mercy, grace, and power in my life. In the name of Jesus.
14. With all that makes You God, let all the enemies of Your prosperity and peace in my life be disgraced and silenced. In the name of Jesus.
15. Wonderful LORD, I thank You for answering these prayers by Your fire. In the name of Jesus.

PRAYER 51

AS YOUR BATTLE AXE AND WEAPON OF WAR, RENEW ME, O LORD!

BIBLE VERSES: *Jeremiah 51:20-23*

INTRODUCTION

A battle axe is an instrument and weapon of war. To be the LORD's battle axe is to be an instrument and weapon of war in the hand of the LORD.

In our Bible verse, the LORD has promised to use His battle axe to accomplish great and mighty works in the world. Therefore, every believer in Christ (the battle axe) is expected to desire and grow into an effective instrument or weapon in the hand of God.

For this reason, there is a need for constant sharpening through the study and meditation in God's Word and fervent prayers. These will nourish the Holy Spirit in the believer to grow into the right stature for effective service.

In line with the expectation of constant renewal, these prayers are designed to dwell more on the psalmist's kind of prayers to equip us for the great task before us. I prophesy, therefore, that all the rust and dirt in your spiritual pipe shall be burnt out by the fire of God and your potency as the LORD's battle axe and weapon of war renewed. In Jesus' mighty name. Amen.

PRAYER POINTS:

1. Mighty and awesome God, I worship You and give glory to Your most holy name for the mighty works You have done in my life.
2. I plead the precious blood of Jesus Christ and cover myself and my family with the blood. In the name of Jesus.
3. Holy Ghost, turn me into Your fire for today's assignment. In the name of Jesus.
4. All the pollution or contamination that came into my life in the dream, be flushed out by the blood of Jesus Christ.
5. Every symptom of weakness or powerlessness in my spiritual life, LORD, wipe out by the blood of Jesus Christ.
6. Spiritual consultants on assignment against my life, receive the arrow of God and die! In the name of Jesus.

7. Spirits of fear and timidity in my life, your time is up. Die by fire! In the name of Jesus.
8. Evil fire, kindled for my sake on the altar of darkness, be blown out by the wind of God. In the name of Jesus.
9. LORD, consume every spirit of infirmity in my life by Your fire. In the name of Jesus.
10. Pass me through Your Refiner's fire, O LORD, and bring me out as gold. In the name of Jesus.
11. Spirits of boldness and sound minds fill me now. In the name of Jesus.
12. Spiritual purity, courage, and availability for divine exploits, possess me by fire. In the name of Jesus.
13. I receive power to tread on serpents and scorpions and over all the power of the Enemy. Nothing shall by any means hurt me. In the name of Jesus.
14. I receive divine authority to terrorize the kingdom of darkness and execute God's judgment on it. In the name of Jesus.
15. LORD, I thank you for answering these prayers by Your fire. In the name of Jesus.

PRAYER 52

OVERRULE AND CANCEL THE JUDGMENT OF THE WICKED OVER MY LIFE, O LORD!

BIBLE VERSE: Psalm 12:5

INTRODUCTION

"Judgment" is the decision or conclusion arrived at after the consideration of facts available in a matter. The "wicked" refers to those who do evil ("wickedly" Daniel 12:10) in action or by intention. God's Word says, "Wickedness proceedeth from the wicked" (1 Samuel 24:13). To do evil is to do wrong things to other people in terms of societal demands or the demands of God in His Word. For the LORD to overrule and cancel the judgment of the wicked in one's life means receiving deliverance from the mighty Redeemer.

The Bible says, "The whole world lieth in wickedness" (1 John 5:19). This means that the world is full of evil and the wicked are the perpetrators of all evil, serving as agents of the dark kingdom with Satan as the head to torment and oppress people in various ways or dimensions. They execute judgment on their victims to frustrate God's plan in their lives. The execution of their judgment often takes the form of direct or indirect attacks on the lives of their victims, which in the final analysis, bring hardship or total elimination.

Believers *must not* be ignorant of Satan's devices (2 Corinthians 2:11). Hence, they must vigorously seek the LORD's face for the judgments of the wicked over our lives to be overruled before they destroy us. I prophesy, therefore, that the LORD shall promptly overrule and cancel the plan, counsel or judgment of the wicked over your life and destiny. In Jesus' mighty name. Amen.

PRAYER POINTS:

1. Great and mighty Redeemer, I thank You for the abundance of Your blessings bestowed upon me. May Your most holy name be praised and honoured forever.

2. I plead the blood of Jesus Christ and cover myself and all that belongs to me with the blood.

3. Any aspect of my life that requires Your mercy, LORD, release it upon me now. In the name of Jesus.

4. Any door that I have opened to the wicked one to arrest and torment my life, LORD, close it by force and Your fire. In the name of Jesus.

5. God, arise and contend with every evil contender in my life and family. In the name of Jesus.

6. LORD, frustrate the desire of the wicked over my life and let them fall by their own wickedness. In the name of Jesus.

7. Let the instrument of death prepared by the wicked for me be turned against them, O LORD. In the name of Jesus.

8. LORD, let the wicked fall into the destruction You have reserved for them. In the name of Jesus.

9. Let the way of the wicked be dark and make them grope in darkness continually, O LORD.

10. God, arise and answer by Your thunder whenever the dark kingdom summons me to their judgment seat in the dream. In the name of Jesus.

11. By the authority of heaven, I command the wicked to fall into the pit they have prepared for me. In the name of Jesus.

12. Mighty Deliverer, overrule and cancel every evil and unrighteous judgment of the wicked over my life and destiny. In the name of Jesus.

13. Let the wickedness of the wicked in my life and family come to an end, O LORD.

14. LORD, clothe me with Your armour of faith and power to quench all the fiery darts of the wicked. In the name of Jesus.
15. LORD, I thank You for answering these prayers by fire. In the name of Jesus.

BOOK BY THE SAME AUTHOR

Sickness, disasters, epidemics, terrorism, kidnappings, financial woes, and witchcraft are all signs of the evil world we live in. Each day, we hear about or confront difficult situations in our homes, workplaces, schools, and even churches.

Will it ever stop?

Are you tired of being pushed around by your enemies?

Can you be happy, healthy, and successful in this wicked world?

Prayer Guide for Spiritual Vitality shows you how. It is a powerful collection of prayers to conquer the evil attacks of the Enemy against you and your family aimed at destruction and perpetual misery. In just a few minutes each day, you can say these potent prayers out loud to restore your physical, spiritual, mental, and financial health.

Your problems are not just physical. They are part of the evil plot from the dark kingdom to destroy your purpose and destiny. But you can win! Take back what has been stolen from you and walk in the freedom God wanted you to have from the day of creation.

This book includes prayers to:

- Get rid of sickness, affliction, suffering, and bondage in you and your family
- Arrange your life and destiny in line with God's original plan
- Restore all the good things, positions, blessings, and rewards that were missed in your life
- Frustrate satanic deceit and manipulations in your life.
- Destroy generational curses, witchcraft, and the conspiracy of the dark kingdom to harm you and your family

www.ingramcontent.com/pod-product-compliance
Lightning Source LLC
Chambersburg PA
CBHW032033290426
44110CB00012B/791